The Writings of Agnes of Harcourt

NOTRE DAME TEXTS IN MEDIEVAL CULTURE

The Writings of

Agnes of Harcourt

The *Life of Isabelle of France* & the *Letter on Louis IX* and *Longchamp*

Edited, translated, and with an Introduction by

Sean L. Field

University of Notre Dame Press · Notre Dame, Indiana

Manufactured in the United States of America

Library of Congress Cataloging-in-Publication Data
Agnes, d'Harcourt, abbesse de Longchamp, d. 1291?
The writings of Agnes of Harcourt : the life of Isabelle of France and
the letter on Louis IX and Longchamp / edited, translated, and with a
historical introduction by Sean L. Field.
p. cm. — (Notre Dame texts in medieval culture)
Includes index.
ISBN 0-268-04403-1 (alk. paper)
ISBN 0-268-04404-x (pbk. : alk. paper)
1. Isabelle, Princess of France, 1225–1270.   2. Princesses—France—Biography.
3. Blessed—France—Biography.   4. Louis IX, King of France, 1214–1270.
5. Abbaye de Longchamp (Paris, France)—History.   I. Field, Sean L. (Sean
Linscott), 1970–   II. Title.   III. Series.
BX4705.I79 A38   2003
282'.44'09022—dc21
2003012369

For my mother and father,

Tamara Myers Field and Larry Francis Field

Contents

Acknowledgments   ix

Introduction   1

1.   The Subject: Isabelle of France   2

2.   The Author: Agnes of Harcourt   3

3.   Dates and Titles of the Texts   9

4.   Historical Context of Agnes's Writings   11

5.   Summary of Contents   20

6.   Manuscripts and Previous Editions   24

7.   Establishment of the Texts   37

8.   Language of the Texts and Translation Principles   40

9.   Reading List   41

Texts

Edition and Translation of the *Letter on Louis IX and Longchamp*   45
     Notes to the Edition and Translation

Edition and Translation of the *Life of Isabelle of France*   51
     Notes to the Edition and Translation

Index   103

Acknowledgments

The research and writing for this book could not have been accomplished without the support of a Fulbright Fellowship for Study in France during 1999/2000 and a Charlotte W. Newcombe Doctoral Dissertation Fellowship in 2001/2002. In Paris I benefited from Alain Boureau's warm welcome to his seminar at the École des Hautes Études en Science Sociale, from illuminating conversations with Nicole Bériou and Jacques Dalarun, and from the help provided by the staffs of the Bibliothèque Nationale de France, the Bibliothèque Mazarine, the Bibiothèque Franciscaine, the Institut de Recherche et d'Histoire des Textes, and the Archives Nationales de France. Even more importantly, my wife, Lori, has offered her understanding, support, and boundless culinary imagination as this project has taken us from Paris to Evanston to Milwaukee, and my daughter Cecilia's smile has made the latter stages of revising the book more enjoyable than I would have thought possible.

Whatever merit this book may have results in large part from the advice and example provided by Robert E. Lerner, who directed the dissertation out of which the project emerged and greatly improved the entire text with his characteristic eye for detail, accuracy, and coherence. I am also very grateful to William Paden for patiently correcting my initial editorial efforts and lending his expert advice on questions of translation, and to Ingrid Muller for her fine work as the book's copyeditor. I claim only my errors as my own. Further thanks are due to Barbara Newman, Richard Kieckhefer, and Ethan Shagan for comments on portions of the introduction, to John Van Engen at the University of Notre Dame Medieval Institute, and to Barbara Hanrahan at the University of Notre Dame Press. I

would also like to thank the Interlibrary Loan staff at the Northwestern University Library for their hard work on my behalf.

It gives me great pleasure to be able to dedicate this book to my mother and father, Tamara and Larry Field, as a small measure of thanks for all the help and encouragement they have given me over many years.

The Writings of Agnes of Harcourt

Introduction

This book is intended to make the important thirteenth-century French writings of Agnes of Harcourt for the first time readily available to scholars and students. Her *Letter on Louis IX and Longchamp* (as I will call this text) has never before appeared in print, and indeed its existence in manuscript has been practically unknown even to specialists. Her *Life of Isabelle of France* was edited once in the seventeenth century, but this early modern edition is now available only in a few rare-book collections and, in any case, was always uncertain in its reliability. An eighteenth-century Latin translation of this edition has been more readily available, but at the price of obscuring Agnes's original French text. Neither of Agnes's works has previously been translated into English.

The most basic information about Agnes of Harcourt's life has not attracted modern scholarly inquiry. A six-page article published by Paulin Paris in the *Histoire littéraire de la France* in 1842 remains the most extensive assessment of Agnes and her work.[1] Unfortunately, much of the information presented by Paris is unreliable. In spite of the recent surge of interest in medieval women as authors, there has been no further study of Agnes or her texts in the intervening century and a half, though presumably twenty-first-century readers will feel even more strongly than their nineteenth-century predecessor that "l'écrit français d'une femme est, au XIIIe siècle, un monument dont il serait aujourd'hui superflu de faire sentir l'importance" (The French writing of a woman in the thirteenth century is a

---

1. Paulin Paris, "Agnès d'Harcourt, abbesse de Longchamp," in *Histoire littéraire de la France*, 20:98–103.

monument the importance of which it would be superfluous to underline today).[2]

The following introduction presents biographical information on Isabelle of France and Agnes of Harcourt, establishes the dates of Agnes's texts, offers an analysis of the context in which she wrote, and summarizes the contents, interest, and importance of her works. Additional introductory material establishes the manuscript tradition of the texts and editorial policies for the present edition. Because most of the information provided here is new, I hope it will be of use to specialists and students alike.

1. The Subject: Isabelle of France

Though much of what we know about Isabelle of France comes from Agnes of Harcourt's writings themselves, we are fortunate that a substantial body of additional evidence allows us to round out our picture of her life. Isabelle was the only sister of one of France's most revered kings, Louis IX, or Saint Louis, as he is better known. Her father, Louis VIII, died shortly after her birth in 1225. Isabelle is initially an interesting figure because of her determined resistance to her family's marriage plans for her. In 1227, while Isabelle was still an infant, her mother, Blanche of Castile, attempted to arrange her future marriage to the son of Hugh of Lusignan and Isabelle of Angoulême, count and countess of La Marche, but the alliance never materialized. More dramatically, in 1243 the emperor Frederick II sought Isabelle's hand for his son and heir, Conrad. Blanche and Louis IX seem to have favored the idea, and Pope Innocent IV even wrote to Isabelle to urge her to accept. But, as it turned out, Isabelle rejected the marriage, successfully asserting her desire to dedicate herself to a life of virginity. Subsequently, both Innocent IV and his successor, Alexander IV, wrote to her to praise her decision and her devout life more generally, demonstrating Isabelle's growing reputation for saintliness.

In the 1250s Isabelle channeled her funds and energies into founding a new house for Franciscan women. The "Abbey of the Humility of Our Lady," or Longchamp, as it quickly became known, was situated just west of Paris, near the Seine, on the western edge of the modern Bois de

---

2. Ibid., 99.

Boulogne, more or less on the site of a horse-race track, which has inherited the name of Longchamp. Isabelle coauthored the first rule for her abbey with an illustrious team of Franciscans including St. Bonaventure, William of Meliton, William of Harcombourg, and her confessor, Eudes of Rosny. All of these men were masters at the University of Paris. This rule was approved by Pope Alexander IV in February 1259, the first nuns entered Longchamp in June 1260, and a revised rule was granted by Pope Urban IV in July 1263. Isabelle herself did not become a nun at her new foundation but constructed a modest residence and chapel on the abbey grounds, where she lived until her death on 23 February 1270, when her tomb at Longchamp became an object of pilgrimage and the site of numerous miracles. In 1521 Pope Leo X belatedly granted Longchamp permission to celebrate Isabelle's office; since that time she has traditionally been known as the "blessed" Isabelle of France.

Isabelle is a fascinating figure in her own right as a second "saint" next to the better-known Saint Louis and as an influential female patron of the Franciscan order. But this inherent interest is greatly amplified by the fact that the richest source for Isabelle's life is one of the very few religious biographies composed by a woman in the Middle Ages, the vernacular *Life of Isabelle* written by her contemporary, the third abbess of Longchamp, Agnes of Harcourt.[3]

2. The Author: Agnes of Harcourt

Her Family

Agnes of Harcourt came from an illustrious Norman noble family, which was increasingly favored by the thirteenth- and early-fourteenth-century Capetians.[4] She was the daughter of Jean I, baron of Harcourt and

---

3. On Isabelle of France see Sean Field, "The Princess, the Abbess, and the Friars: Isabelle of France and the Course of Thirteenth-Century Religious History" (Ph.D. diss., Northwestern University, 2002), and Field, "New Evidence for the Life of Isabelle of France," *Revue Mabillon*, n.s., 13 (2002): 109–123. For further secondary literature on Isabelle of France and Agnes of Harcourt see the reading list at the end of this introduction.

4. Most accounts of the Harcourt family in the thirteenth century are ultimately based on Gilles-André de la Roque, *Histoire généalogique de la maison de Harcourt*, 4 vols. (Paris,

vicomte of St. Sauveur. Best known for his military exploits, Jean I fought on crusades with Louis IX in 1270 and Philip III in 1285, before his death in 1288. Agnes's mother was Alix of Beaumont, who probably married Jean around 1240 and died in 1275.

The brothers of the family could boast an impressive résumé of military, ecclesiastical, and political success. Jean II of Harcourt added to his father's titles those of field marshal and admiral of France. The younger Jean accompanied his father on the crusades of 1270 and 1285 and died in 1302 on a Sicilian expedition, following Charles of Valois, the brother of King Philip IV. A trio of Agnes's brothers reached a similar level of eminence within the church and as counselors to the later Capetians. Raoul, Robert, and Guy of Harcourt were, respectively, archdeacon of Coutance and Rouen, bishop of Coutance, and bishop of Lisieux, as well as the founders of the College of Harcourt and the College of Lisieux in Paris. They were among Philip III's and Philip IV's advisors, engaging in diplomatic missions on their behalf and appearing at their councils.

The Harcourt family's ties to Longchamp were strong from the abbey's very inception. One of Jean I of Harcourt's sisters, Jeanne "the elder," joined Agnes among the original group of women to take the veil at Longchamp in 1260. Agnes's sister Jeanne became a nun at Longchamp in 1277, followed Agnes as abbess from 26 April 1294 to 17 February 1299, and died 1 November 1315. Jean I of Harcourt appears in Longchamp's records in July 1281, when he made a donation of rents to the abbey on behalf of the younger Jeanne.[5]

In sum, Agnes's immediate family formed a network of interlocking military, political, and ecclesiastical influence. Her father and eldest brother were the companions of kings on crusades and military expeditions, and

---

1662), esp. 1:324–349, 2:1724–1776, 3:186–232, and 4:1189–1239. On Agnes see 2:1775 and 4:1236-1239. More recently (though not necessarily more accurately) see Georges Martin, *Histoire et généalogie de la maison de Harcourt* (La Ricamarie, 1974), 61–66. Léopold Delisle sheds more reliable light on some aspects of the thirteenth-century history of the Harcourt family in his *Histoire du Chateau et des Sires Saint-Sauveur-le-Vicomte* (Paris and Caen, 1867). The present discussion is a condensed version of chapter 7 of Field, "The Princess, the Abbess, and the Friars," where more detailed documentation on Agnes and her family can be found.

5. The original grant is Archives Nationales de France (hereafter AN) K35, no. 4.

her other brothers were rising through the ranks of the church just as Agnes and her sister were achieving more localized power as abbesses of Longchamp. It is thus useful to keep in mind that Agnes of Harcourt was a well-connected noblewoman from a powerful family, as well as a nun and abbess.

Agnes of Harcourt's Career

There is no concrete evidence for the date of Agnes's birth. Since her parents probably married around 1240 and Agnes was serving as abbess of Longchamp by the mid-1260s, it seems most probable that she was born in the early or mid-1240s. It is traditionally said that Agnes was a lady-in-waiting in the household of Isabelle of France.[6] Though there is little direct evidence for this claim, a close reading of her *Life of Isabelle* does seem to reveal that her personal memories of Isabelle began before Longchamp's founding in 1260, indicating that Agnes probably did follow Isabelle from life at court to the new royal abbey.

Agnes was certainly among the original group of women to enter Longchamp in June 1260, and within a few years she was elected abbess. Most older scholarship gives the dates of her abbacy as 1263–1279.[7] However, the extant archival evidence establishes that this tradition is incorrect. It was the custom at Longchamp for each incoming abbess to compile an inventory of the abbey's possessions and to reconcile its accounts. These inventories and accounts were then sewn together into rolls for reference and safekeeping. The surviving account rolls from the 1270s and 1280s reveal previous assertions as to the dates of Agnes's abbacy to be demonstrably false.

Agnes served two different terms as abbess of Longchamp. The exact dates of her first term are difficult to pin down. They certainly covered at a minimum the years 1266 to 1270. Based on evidence for the terms of the other women known to have served as abbesses in Longchamp's earliest

---

6. This tradition goes back at least to a book of 1619 that referred to Agnes as "cete devote Moniale, ancienne Domestique de la Saincte [Isabelle of France]." Sébastien Roulliard, *La Saincte Mère, ou Vie de M. Saincte Isabel de France, soeur unique du Roy S. Louis, fondatrice de l'Abbaye de Long-champ* (Paris, 1619), 448.

7. For example, *Gallia Christiana*, vol. 7 (1744), col. 945, following Roulliard, says Agnes's abbacy started in 1263 and lasted seventeen years. Similarly Gaston Duchesne, *Histoire de l'abbaye royale de Longchamp (1255 à 1789)*, 2d ed. (Paris, 1906), 119, gives the dates as February 1263 to February 1279.

years, it seems probable that Agnes's first term lasted about eleven years, from approximately 1264 to 1275.[8] Her second term in office, however, is definitely dated by the surviving accounts as 2 September 1281 to 29 August 1287.[9]

---

8. AN L1020, no. 26A, and J148, no. 6, were issued by Agnes as abbess in 1266 and 1267 (see Field, "The Princess, the Abbess, and the Friars," chap. 7, nn. 41 and 42, for transcriptions), and Agnes herself reveals in miracle twelve of her *Life of Isabelle* that she was abbess when Isabelle of France died in February 1270. In 1260, Longchamp's first year of existence, Isabelle of Venice of Reims served as the abbey's president, and there was no abbess. The first two true abbesses of Longchamp (Agnes of Anery and Mahaut of Guyencourt) probably served short terms between 1261 and 1264 or 1265, when Agnes's first term would have begun. Agnes's first term must have ended around 1275, because the term of the fourth abbess, Julianne of Troyes, came before 1278 (see note 9). See Field, "The Princess, the Abbess, and the Friars," 278–280 and appendix G (forthcoming in *Archivum Franciscanum Historicum* 96 [2003] as "The Abbesses of Longchamp up to the Black Death") for the archival evidence on which these conclusions are based.

9. See Field, "The Princess, the Abbess, and the Friars," appendix G for a summary of all evidence for the dates of the abbesses of Longchamp up to 1348. Sister Jehanne of Nevers served as Longchamp's fifth abbess from 24 February 1278 to 2 September 1281, at which date Agnes of Harcourt began her second term, which lasted until 29 August 1287, according to the contemporary account roll AN L1026, no. 1bis: "En l'an de l'incarnation Nostre Seigneur m.cc. lxxix. Le jour saint Maci commenca la tierce anné l'abbesse suer J. de Nevers." Since this date (February 1280 new style) began her third year as abbess, Jehanne's term began in 1278. Her entry in the 1325 necrology (Molinier, *Obituaires*, 666) confirms that she was the fifth to serve as abbess: "S. Jehanne de Nevers, LX [sixtieth nun to die]. Elle fu la quinte abbeesse, et le fu par iii fois. A la S. Mathieu en septembre [her date of death]." For the beginning of Agnes of Harcourt's term, AN L1026, no. 2, states: "L'an de grace .m.cc. iiii[xx]. & i, Le mardi devant la feste Nostre Dame en septembre seur Agnus de Harcourt recuit l'office d'abbesse et seur Jehenne de Nevers fu assote de l'office." Moreover, AN L1026, no. 3, is a fragment of the "recetes et despnes de sixime anee l'abbesse s. Agnes de Harecourt l'an de grace mil duo cens quatre vins et six," which began "le mercredi devant la feste Nostre Dame en septembre" (Cocheris, *Histoire de la ville, et de tout le diocèse de Paris par l'Abbé Lebeuf. Nouvelle édition annotée et continuée jusqu'à nos jours par Hippolyte Cocheris*, vol. 4, [Paris, 1870], 260–261). For the end of Agnes's term, AN L1026, no. 4, states: "L'an de grace .m.cc. iiii[xx] et vii, recetes et despense du premier an l'abbeesse seur Jehenne de Grece qui commenca le jeudi qui fu jours saint Jehan decollace et fina y ce memes jour l'an retuurnet." (There is a problem here for which I cannot account, in that St. John Decollation day, August 29, was on Friday in 1287.) Also in AN L1026, no. 2: "L'an de grace mil cc iiii[xx] et vii que seur J. de Grece recuit l'office d'abbeesse et seur Agnes de Harcourt fu assote." This confirms that Agnes of Harcourt was abbess in December 1282 when she wrote her *Letter on Louis IX and Longchamp*.

Most secondary sources give 25 November 1289 or 1291 as the date of Agnes's death. In fact, Longchamp's first necrology indicates that she was the nineteenth nun to die and gives the day of her death as 25 November, but does not specify the year. Since a document extant in the Archives Nationales de France demonstrates that Agnes was still alive in March 1290, perhaps 25 November 1291 is the most likely date for her death.[10]

What do we know of Agnes as an abbess? She seems to have been a particularly active and energetic leader of her community. Her importance to her monastic house should already be apparent from the chronological outline presented above—Agnes was the first abbess to serve for an extended period, solidifying Longchamp's leadership for a decade after three different women had headed the house in the first four or five years of its existence. Similarly, she was the first sister to be reelected to the office, perhaps indicating that after a few years in the 1270s the nuns felt the need to return to an experienced leader. All told she was abbess for about seventeen of the house's first twenty-seven years and thus a driving force behind its early development.

Longchamp's inventories from the early fourteenth century mention three books that had once belonged to Agnes. The inventory of 1305 mentions "one great book of sermons that was Agnes of Harcourt's."[11] Though it is unfortunate that we do not know what sort of collection this was, whether it was in Latin or French, or how Agnes acquired it, the simple

---

10. As mentioned above, Jean I of Harcourt gave rents to Longchamp for his daughter Jeanne in July 1281. One of the later confirmations of the grant is AN K34, no. 4[2bis]. On the back of this document is written "Mars 1289 Sr. Agnes d'Harcourt," (March 1289, Sister Agnes of Harcourt), indicating that she was still alive to have documents directed to her attention at that date. But since this date would be reckoned as March 1290 in modern terms, we can be confident that Agnes did not die in November 1289. (Easter fell on 10 April in 1289, and 2 April in 1290. Thus the month of March falling between these dates would have been considered the end of 1289 according to the thirteenth-century Parisian custom of beginning the new year with Easter.) On the other hand, it seems doubtful (though admittedly not impossible) that Jeanne of Harcourt (the younger) would have been elected abbess in April 1294 if her older sister had still been alive and active. Thus Agnes probably died on 25 November between 1290 and 1293, and the traditional date of approximately 1291 seems acceptable.

11. AN K37, no. 2. Edited in *Cocheris, Histoire de la ville,* 4:263.

possession of such a book indicates her familiarity with religious writings. The inventory of 1325 also mentions a missal and a collectionary that had belonged to Agnes.[12] These sorts of liturgical books were unremarkable possessions for a nun, to be sure, but provide further evidence for Agnes's habits as a reader and book owner.

The extant archival evidence reveals Agnes as an abbess who worked through legal channels, royal influence (no doubt side by side with Isabelle of France), and negotiation with other monastic houses to protect and increase Longchamp's lands and income. These documents show Agnes and Longchamp successfully filing a legal claim to see that the terms of a will were enforced, buying land, negotiating for properties and rents with the Monasteries of St. Denis, St. Geneviève, St. Victor, and Joyenval, and securing royal privileges and confirmations of earlier acquisitions.[13]

Moreover, Agnes of Harcourt occupies a unique position in Longchamp's early records in several notable ways. Close to one hundred documents dating from the earliest purchases for Longchamp's foundation through the end of the thirteenth century survive in the Archives Nationales de France. Yet in all of these documents, Agnes of Harcourt is the only abbess ever mentioned by name in legal records or to have issued surviving documents in her own name. Similarly, she is the only abbess of Longchamp before the middle of the fourteenth century for whom a seal is extant.[14]

Agnes of Harcourt thus emerges from these physical artifacts as a woman with a public presence unlike other thirteenth-century abbesses of Longchamp who are known only through the abbey's internal records. We are left with the impression of an abbess more literate, more adept at dealing with written documents, and more forceful in legal matters than her contemporaries.

---

12. AN L1027, no. 5.

13. AN L1020, nos. 20, 22, 23, 26–30, 32, 33, 35. Similar documents from this period recording land transactions and royal confirmations include AN K32, nos. 5, 7–12; K33, nos. 5, 8, 11; and J148, no. 6.

14. AN J148, no. 6. A reproduction of Agnes's seal from this document can be consulted in the sigillography room at the Archives Nationales de France; for a description see Louis Douët d'Arcq, *Collection de sceaux*, vol. 3 (Paris, 1868), no. 9221.

3. Dates and Titles of the Texts

The *Letter on Louis IX and Longchamp*

Of Agnes of Harcourt's two important texts, the first is a short letter or attestation. Since it is addressed simply to "all who will see this letter," it is not an example of personal correspondence between two people such as the modern use of the word "letter" would imply. It is rather a document intended to preserve a record of Agnes's and her nuns' memories. Nevertheless, "letter" seems the simplest term with which to designate this text, and I have elected to refer to it as Agnes of Harcourt's *Letter on Louis IX and Longchamp* in order to accurately reflect its contents, which will be discussed below. There is no difficulty in determining when it was written, since it is dated 4 December 1282.

The *Life of Isabelle of France*

The second and more substantial text to be considered here is Agnes's biography of Isabelle of France. If we were to follow strictly Agnes's designation in the first line of the text, it should properly be called *La vie de notre saincte et benoite dame et mere Madame Yzabeau de France,* or "The Life of Our Holy and Blessed Lady and Mother Madame Isabelle of France." But for simplicity's sake this biography will here be referred to simply as Agnes of Harcourt's *Life of Isabelle of France.* The date of this *Life* has never been firmly established in any printed work, though this task can be accomplished with a fair degree of accuracy and certainty.

The *Life* was obviously written after Isabelle's death in February 1270 and before Agnes's death around 1291, but internal textual evidence and external circumstances suggest a more exact dating. The initial sentence of the text establishes that Agnes wrote at the request of Isabelle's brother, Charles of Anjou, king of Sicily. Charles's death on 7 January 1285 therefore gives an earlier terminus for the text's composition. Moreover, the possibility that the *Life of Isabelle* was commissioned before 1285 but not actually composed until later is nullified by Agnes's indication that Philip III was king at the time of her writing, since Philip died shortly after Charles on

5 October 1285.[15] Other internal evidence points to a date after 1280. Enough time had passed since Isabelle's death for the advent of numerous posthumous miracles. Most specifically, one sister healed of a fever by drinking from a goblet used by Isabelle is said (in miracle fourteen) to have been well for over ten years. Thus the internal evidence of the *Life* argues for a date between 1280 and 1285.

The movements of Charles of Anjou within this time frame narrow the possibilities still further. Charles left France in 1265 in order to accept a papal invitation to become king of Sicily.[16] He did not return until April of 1283, when he spent several months in Paris at the court of Philip III. After traveling to Bordeaux and Provence, he was again briefly in Paris at the end of the same year, but then departed for good.[17] It seems very probable that one of these Parisian sojourns gave him the opportunity to suggest that Agnes set down the deeds of his holy sister.

Agnes of Harcourt therefore began her *Life of Isabelle* in or shortly after 1283, perhaps only a few months after the composition of the *Letter on Louis IX and Longchamp*, and must have completed it by the beginning of 1285.

---

15. Miracle seventeen relates that "Madame the great Queen Marguerite, mother of the King of France, had Monseigneur Philip, the son of the king, brought [to Isabelle's tomb]. . . ." Marguerite of Provence was the wife of Louis IX, hence mother of Philip III, who was king at this moment, and grandmother of Philip IV, who was evidently not yet king.

16. Charles's movements are traced in Paul Durrieu, *Les Archives Angevines de Naples: Étude sur les registres du roi Charles Ier (1265–1285)*, vol. 2 (Paris, 1886–1887), 165–189. For recent assessments of Charles see Jean Dunbabin, *Charles I of Anjou: Power, Kingship, and State-Making in Thirteenth-Century Europe* (London and New York, 1998), and David Abulafia, "Charles of Anjou Reassessed," *Journal of Medieval History* 26 (2000): 93–114.

17. Durrieu, *Les Archives Angevines de Naples*, 188–189. Charles left Sicily in January 1282, traveled across Italy during February, and was definitely in Paris during May, probably somewhat earlier. Charles returned to Paris in December 1283 and departed in January 1284. See also Le Comte Riant, "Déposition de Charles d'Anjou pour la Canonisation de Saint Louis," in *Notices et Documents publiés par la Société de l'histoire de France à l'occasion du cinquantième anniversaire de sa fondation* (Paris, 1884), 162 and 162 n. 1, who says that Charles was in Paris in August 1283.

4. Historical Context of Agnes's Writings

Capetian Sanctity

In light of the evidence that locates Agnes of Harcourt's texts in 1282–1283, we can reconstruct the scenario that led her to take up her pen. The initial impulse for Agnes's texts was wrapped up in the canonization proceedings for Louis IX, the future Saint Louis.

On 22 February 1281, overawed by Charles of Anjou's troops, the College of Cardinals elected Simon of Brie as Pope Martin IV.[18] The new pope was a Frenchman who had acted as counselor and then papal legate at the court of Louis IX, where in 1263 he had handled both the negotiations that led to Charles of Anjou's acceptance of the throne of Sicily and the papal approval of Isabelle's revised rule of 1263 for the nuns of Longchamp. Simon of Brie was therefore keenly attuned to Capetian political and religious ambitions. Moreover, his election as pope placed one of the key figures in previous inquiries into Louis's sanctity in a position to give these proceedings a new impetus. After Louis IX's death in 1270, Pope Gregory X had asked Simon to begin a secret investigation into Louis's merits for sainthood. But, unfortunately, by the time Simon finished his initial inquiry in early 1276, Gregory had just died and the process was then further derailed by the rapid elections and deaths of Popes Innocent V, Adrian V, and John XXI. In 1278 Pope Nicholas III put Simon in charge of a new preliminary public inquest into Louis's case. After his own election, therefore, Martin IV had a well-established interest in seeing Louis's canonization accomplished. On his ascension to the papacy Martin directed the archbishop of Rouen and the bishops of Auxerre and Spoleto to gather and verify information on Louis's life and miracles. This investigation, carried out at the monastery of St. Denis (just north of Paris) between May 1282 and March 1283, assembled more than 330 witnesses, resulting in the approval of some sixty miracles attributed to Louis.[19] Though Louis was not

---

18. On Charles of Anjou's role in Martin IV's election, see Steven Runciman, *The Sicilian Vespers* (Cambridge, 1958), 190–191.

19. The summary presented in this paragraph relies on Louis Carolus-Barré, *Le Procès de canonisation de Saint Louis (1272–1297): Essai de reconstitution*, ed. Henri Platelle (Rome, 1994), 2–23.

actually canonized until August 1297, it was the gathering of testimony in 1282–1283 under Martin IV that provided the body of evidence necessary for his ultimate official recognition as a saint.

Thus Agnes of Harcourt's *Letter on Louis IX and Longchamp*, dated 4 December 1282, was written while this inquiry into Louis's merits was going on at St. Denis. This date might well be taken as a coincidence, proving nothing about Agnes's intentions or motivations, but for a fact that has up to now gone unrecognized: the subject of Agnes's letter of December 1282 was not primarily Isabelle of France but Louis IX and his involvement with Longchamp. A brief outline of the text will serve to prove the point. After the greeting, the first sentence commences, "We make known to all who will see this letter that our very reverend and holy father, Monseigneur the king Louis, founded our church and with his own hand placed its first stone at the foundation." This introduction establishes the purpose of the letter—to set down Louis's role as Longchamp's benefactor and to detail his relations with the abbey. To this end, the letter next recalls that "[o]ur same very reverend and holy father, Monseigneur the king Louis, was most devoutly present when we entered into religion and enclosed us," and then goes on to add that he came to a chapter meeting of the nuns, expounded the first sermon and teaching they received, and exhorted them to live up to the models of St. Francis and St. Clare in order to set an example for other nuns. The rest of the text adds further information on Louis's actions toward Longchamp. He would attend the sick and check on the sisters' food supply on his visits. He came to Isabelle of France's burial and even guarded the door to keep out unwanted intruders. When he left for his (second) crusade, he again entered the nuns' chapter meeting and asked for their prayers. "And," adds the letter, "many of us firmly believe that he cured us of fevers and other great maladies." Finally, the letter notes the gifts of relics, building materials, rents, and firewood that the king provided.

At every turn the subject of the letter is Louis—Louis founds the church, Louis enters among the nuns to preach, Louis attends his sister's funeral, Louis cures the sick, Louis gives generous gifts. In short, this letter is in essence a testimony to Louis IX's sanctity, complete with miraculous cures. It was written down at Longchamp just as the main inquiry into Louis's merits was in full swing on the other side of Paris, at St. Denis. It would be difficult to believe that these two facts were unrelated. Though hard evidence is lacking to show that the testimony of Agnes's *Letter* actu-

ally made it into the now lost official records of the commissioners, it seems likely that it was conceived of as a deposition.[20] Thus, Agnes's *Letter on Louis IX and Longchamp* should be seen as a "new" addition to the dossier of St. Louis's canonization process, or at the very least as intimately related to and inspired by the inquiry of 1282–1283.

The fact that Agnes wrote the *Life of Isabelle* at the request of Charles of Anjou has already been noted as evidence that the work was probably begun between April and December of 1283. But why did Charles make this request? His commission was rather uncommon; whereas texts composed by men at the request of women proliferated throughout the Middle Ages, the reverse was unusual.[21] On a general level, Charles was closely involved in the push for Louis's canonization and presumably saw an opportunity to build up the notion of a wider Capetian sanctity by publicizing his sister's sanctity as well. André Vauchez has noted the unabashed manner in which Charles presented his family as a *beata stirps*, or holy lineage, in which sanctity flowed through the royal blood.[22] Charles played an

20. Louis IX's seventeenth-century biographer, Sébastien le Nain de Tillemont, seems to have viewed it as such, although his observation on the subject has not received much notice from more recent historians. In his *Vie de saint Louis, roi de France*, ed. J. de Gaulle, vol. 5, (Paris, 1847–1851), 217, discussing the remnants of Louis's canonization process, he states, "Nous avons la déposition de l'abbesse et des religieuses de Longchamp, datée du 2 décembre 1282, où elles marquent ce que saint Louis avoit fait dans leur monastère, et témoignent que plusieurs d'entre elles croyoient avoir esté guéries par luy de diverses maladies," citing his manuscript B. Presumably a careless copy is to be blamed for Tillemont giving the date as 2 December rather than 4 (two days before the nones of) December. See below on Tillemont, his work, and his manuscript B. But since Agnes's *Letter* has never been edited and Tillemont's copy is no longer found in his manuscript B (BNF. ms. fr. 13747), Tillemont's characterization of this text as a "déposition" has not made an impression on more recent scholars of St. Louis and his canonization process, nor is Agnes mentioned in Carolus-Barré's fine work.

21. On women's roles as commissioners of texts see Joan M. Ferrante, *To the Glory of Her Sex: Women's Roles in the Composition of Medieval Texts* (Bloomington, IN, 1997), 39–135.

22. André Vauchez, *La Sainteté en occident aux derniers siècles du Moyen Age* (Rome, 1981), 214. Translated by Jean Birrell as *Sainthood in the Later Middle Ages* (Cambridge, 1997), 182. On the far-reaching consequences of Charles's quest for *"la sainteté du lignage"* see Gábor Klaniczay, "The Cult of Dynastic Saints in Central Europe: Fourteenth-Century Angevins and Luxemburgs," in *The Uses of Supernatural Power*, trans. Susan Singerman, ed. Karen Margolis (Cambridge, 1990), 111–128, and Klaniczay, *Holy Rulers and Blessed*

important role in reviving efforts to have Louis IX declared a saint, first by ensuring the election of a compliant pope, and then with his own testimony in the canonization process, which he probably gave while still in Italy in early 1282.[23]

Charles's testimony displays a marked desire to create a holy aura around his entire family, beginning with his description of his mother's exemplary death in the habit of a Cistercian nun. To Charles, his mother, Blanche of Castile, was the saintly root from which had sprung the equally saintly branches Louis, Robert, and Alphonse, all of whom he considered martyrs to the faith.[24] But he also included Isabelle in his vision of Capetian sanctity. He emphasized that Blanche watched over and brought up not only Louis but also his brothers and his sister with care and diligence after the death of Louis VIII.[25] A more pointed reference occurs in Guillaume of Saint-Pathus's biography of Louis (c. 1303), which relied on the testimony of the 1282–1283 investigation and quoted Charles directly as stating that Robert, Alphonse, and Isabelle were people of such purity and chastity that he had never heard anyone accuse them of committing a mortal sin and that certainly they, along with Louis, had had the grace of God until the end of their lives.[26] A desire to see his sister's sanctity publicly proclaimed was a logical extension of this testimony.

But if Charles of Anjou was demonstrably interested in promoting the sanctity of his family members, including his sister, one might still ask why he turned to Agnes, rather than perhaps to a learned Franciscan associated with Longchamp, to carry out the proposed biography of his sister. One might respond that Agnes was the abbess of Isabelle's foundation and hence a logical choice. But a more specific answer suggests itself—Charles

---

Princesses: Dynastic Cults in Medieval Central Europe, trans. Éva Pálmai (Cambridge, 2002), 295–331.

23. Charles probably gave his deposition directly to Cardinal Benedict Gaietani (who, as Boniface VIII, would eventually declare Louis's canonization in 1297) when the two met at Naples in February of 1282. Le Comte Riant, "Déposition de Charles d'Anjou pour la Canonisation de Saint Louis," 163.

24. Carolus-Barré, *Le Procès de canonisation de Saint Louis*, 75.

25. Ibid., 68.

26. H.-François Delaborde, *Vie de Saint Louis par Guillaume de Saint-Pathus, confesseur de la Reine Marguerite* (Paris, 1899), 132.

may well have seen a copy of Agnes's December 1282 *Letter on Louis IX and Longchamp*. Encountering Agnes's testimony of Louis and Isabelle acting together in pious endeavors might have raised the idea in Charles's mind of expanding his campaign for Capetian sanctity to include his sister. Turning to the *Letter*'s author would then be a natural step, since Agnes had already demonstrated both her position close to Isabelle and her skills as an author.

In sum, Agnes of Harcourt's authorial career commenced in the context of Louis IX's canonization process and then moved to promote the idea of Isabelle as a saint as well. This move was encouraged by Charles of Anjou as part of his vision of his family's sanctity. The *Life of Isabelle of France* is thus closely linked to a general drive for recognition of Capetian sanctity.

Intended Audiences for the *Life of Isabelle of France*

Within this push for Capetian sanctity, Agnes and the nuns of Longchamp had their own reasons for wanting to see Isabelle's merits recognized along with Louis's. Agnes's own explanation of her motivations is contained in the first sentence of the work: "We have proposed to write the life of our holy and blessed lady and mother, Madame Isabelle of France, at the request of Monseigneur the King of Sicily, her full brother, in so far as God will grant us his grace, for the honor of our Lord Jesus Christ and of this blessed saint and for the edification of the Holy Church." The justification is quite simply Charles's request, and the purpose is to honor Isabelle and provide edification for readers. But while a life of their founder would certainly have offered instructive reading and listening material for the nuns of Longchamp, as the *Life* unfolds, this sort of internal use does not always seem to have been uppermost in Agnes's mind. Promoting Isabelle's cult was in Longchamp's interest in at least three ways, pointing to multiple intended audiences for the *Life* outside the abbey.

First, Agnes constructed the *Life of Isabelle* with an eye to future official papal canonization proceedings, probably with the image of the recent papal inquiry into Louis IX's merits still fresh in her mind. A preliminary *vita* compiled on local initiative and marshaling local testimony on a prospective saint's virtues, reputation for sanctity, and posthumous miracles was generally the first step in petitioning the papal Curia to open official

canonization proceedings in the thirteenth century.[27] The support of influential local leaders or preferably the royal court was necessary if an initial appeal of this sort was to make progress, but Agnes and the nuns of Longchamp could reasonably have expected Charles of Anjou and the royal family to offer this aid. The next step would have been an official designation of papal commissioners to launch a formal inquiry, but Isabelle's cause never got that far. Indeed, no copy of Agnes's *Life* was ever actually sent to Rome, so far as we know.

Nevertheless, the *Life* is constructed with this sort of potential future process in mind. Wherever possible, Agnes cites specific witnesses who can testify to the *Life*'s claims. For instance, in a story in which Isabelle insists that she had been just as devout when she wore fine clothes as she would later be in simpler dress, Agnes not only stresses that Isabelle related this information to her "with her own mouth," but goes on to say that "I believe that there will be others who will certainly testify to this if need be." The phrase "if need be" evokes an envisioned future hearing into Isabelle's merits where additional witnesses could be called to corroborate Agnes's personal testimony. Similarly, many of the miraculous cures worked at Isabelle's tomb are vouched for by specific surviving nuns, mentioned by name.

The *Life* has a royal audience in mind as well. This purpose is revealed more clearly when Agnes's activities as a biographer are seen as emerging from her *Letter* detailing Louis's involvement with Longchamp. Whereas the *Letter* had satisfactorily established the king's role in helping to found Longchamp, the *Life* detailed the contributions of the abbey's other royal patron. Together, the two works would serve to remind Louis's and Isabelle's successors of established Capetian favor for Longchamp. Agnes emphasizes Isabelle's royal lineage at the outset of the work, tracing her ancestry back to her grandfathers, Philip Augustus of France and Alfonso VIII of Castile. By invoking members of the royal family as witnesses and sources of information, Agnes makes the Capetian court part of her project. These royal sources include Louis, his wife Marguerite of Provence, and their grandson, the future Philip IV. At second hand, through Isabelle's childhood nurse Helen de Buisemont, Agnes also reports the recollections of

---

27. Vauchez, *Sainthood in the Later Middle Ages*, 40–43. A life composed in French would presumably have been translated into Latin and probably revised by a clerical supporter before it reached Rome.

Blanche of Castile. The second half of the *Life*, describing Isabelle's post-humous miracles, may have been just as important for this purpose. This section not only put forth the miraculous element of Isabelle's claim to sainthood, but demonstrated to the royal family Isabelle's continued presence at her tomb at Longchamp. In particular, the *Life* reminded the future Philip IV that he owed his very survival to Isabelle's intercession.

Finally, the *Life* was intended to spread Isabelle's fame among potential pilgrims, using the early miracles at Isabelle's grave as self-perpetuating publicity. This function of the text is clearest in the section on miracles worked for women from the region. For instance, Agnes "the chest maker" had an ailing child whom she loved very much but who was expected to die. She fell asleep and heard a voice say, "Agnes, dedicate your child to Madame Isabelle, near St. Cloud, and offer her the cup that your father gave you, and your child will be cured!" As a result, "[t]he next day she came to our house on pilgrimage and offered the cup, and the child was cured." Another woman, also named Agnes, had gone blind. But after being brought to Longchamp and dedicating herself to Isabelle and promising the saint two eyes made of wax, her sight was restored. These stories and the several that follow not only report miraculous healings, they provide a road map for future pilgrims. This map is quite literal in so far as the voices the sufferers hear are always careful to mention that Isabelle's abbey can be found near St. Cloud (now on the southwest edge of Paris), providing physical direction to the abbey. More generally, with these stories potential pilgrims are instructed that the proper course of action if they hope to be healed or saved in some way is to make a physical pilgrimage to Longchamp, dedicate themselves to Isabelle, and make an offering.

Women's Writing and Vernacular Hagiography in the Thirteenth Century

Agnes was part of a long tradition of medieval female authors that includes such famous names as Hildegard of Bingen, Heloise, and Marie de France.[28] But the thirteenth century unquestionably saw a new flowering of

---

28. For a good introduction see Peter Dronke, *Women Writers of the Middle Ages: A Critical Study of Texts from Perpetua (d. 203) to Marguerite Porete (d. 1310)* (Cambridge, 1984). It is indicative of the general scholarly neglect of Agnes of Harcourt that she receives no mention at all in Dronke's text or in his extensive bibliography of female writers.

vernacular religious works written by women. Agnes of Harcourt should be seen as a contributor to the emergence of this literature.

Of the great thirteenth-century "Beguine mystics," those who wrote in Dutch and German vernaculars predated Agnes. Hadewijch of Brabant wrote her Dutch poems, letters, and visions in the period around 1220–1240, while Beatrice of Nazareth (c. 1200–1268), a Cistercian who had close contact with Beguine communities, similarly composed her Dutch *Seven Manners of Loving* several decades before Agnes's works. Mechthild of Magdeburg (c. 1208–c. 1282 or c. 1297) began her Middle-Low-German *Flowing Light of the Godhead* in the 1250s and continued adding to it until the last years of her life. But the outstanding contributor to this genre in the French language, Marguerite Porete (d. 1310), probably did not begin her *Mirror of Simple Souls* until about 1296, more than a decade after Agnes took up her pen.[29]

The rise of the mendicant orders contributed to the new prominence for women's writing in the thirteenth century, already exemplified by the Dominican-influenced Mechthild of Magdeburg. If one looks at thirteenth-century female authors through a specifically Franciscan lens, Agnes of Harcourt wrote somewhat later than St. Clare (1194–1253), but was a contemporary of Angela of Foligno (c. 1248–1309), who did not begin to dictate her work until about 1290. Both of these Italian women wrote (or, in Angela's case, had their works written down) in Latin. But, as the great German historian Herbert Grundmann long ago pointed out, Agnes's work is the first example of vernacular religious literature authored by a woman associated with the Franciscans (or Dominicans, for that matter) in northern France.[30] Indeed, this claim can be extended to southern France as well,

---

29. Useful surveys of this literature are Elizabeth Petroff, ed., *Medieval Women's Visionary Literature* (New York and Oxford, 1986), and Katherina Wilson, ed., *Medieval Women Writers* (Athens, GA, 1984). On the Beguine mystics and for a further bibliography see Bernard McGinn, ed., *Meister Eckhart and the Beguine Mystics: Hadwijch of Brabant, Mechthild of Magdeburg, and Marguerite Porete* (New York, 1994), and Amy Hollywood, *The Soul as Virgin Wife* (Notre Dame and London, 1995). On the date of Marguerite's text, see Robert E. Lerner, *The Heresy of the Free Spirit in the Later Middle Ages* (Berkeley and Los Angeles, 1972), 71.

30. Herbert Grundmann, *Religious Movements in the Middle Ages: The Historical Links between Heresy, the Mendicant Orders, and the Women's Religious Movement in the Twelfth and Thirteenth Century, with the Historical Foundations of German Mysticism*, trans. Steven Rowan, introduction by Robert E. Lerner (Notre Dame and London, 1996), 393 n. 44.

since the vernacular Provençal life of the Franciscan-inspired Beguine Douceline of Digne was probably not written by Felipa of Porcellet until 1297.[31]

Agnes's biographical writings are far removed from the mystical texts of Hadewijch, Mechthild, Marguerite, and Angela, and from Clare's mainly didactic writings. The most specific context for Agnes's works is within the genre of female-authored vernacular hagiography. Though female hagiographers were rare in the Middle Ages, they were not unknown.[32] But Agnes's *Life of Isabelle* does seem to have a claim to primacy within the realm of French literature. Clemence of Barking's *Vie de Sainte Catherine* (c. 1180), a life of Edward the Confessor by either Clemence or another nun of Barking (c. 1163–1170), and a thirteenth-century *Vie Seinte Audrée* by a woman named Marie (possibly Marie de France) are examples of earlier vernacular saints' lives by women. These works differ from Agnes of Harcourt's *Life of Isabelle*, however, in that they are translations and reworkings of the Latin lives of earlier Christian saints rather than freshly composed biographies of personal acquaintances. Moreover, they were written in England, mainly in Anglo-Norman dialect, and in verse rather than prose.[33] Among

---

31. First edited with modern French translation in J.-H. Albenés, *La Vie de Sainte Douceline, fondatrice des Béguines de Marseille* (Marseille, 1879). On the date of the text, see pp. xx–xxv, for the author pp. xxv–xxxix. Corrected edition and modern French translation in R. Gout, *La Vie de Sainte Douceline: Texte provençal du XIVe siècle* (Paris, 1927). The most recent edition, with an English translation, is Kathryn Betts Wolfkiel, *"The Life of the Blessed Saint Doucelina* (d. 1274): An Edition and Translation with Commentary" (Ph.d. diss., Northwestern University, 1993). A very welcome English translation is now more readily available in Kathleen Garay and Madeleine Jeay, eds., *The Life of St. Douceline, a Beguine of Provence* (Rochester, NY, 2002).

32. In the early–seventh century the nun Baudonivia wrote a life of the Frankish queen Radegund, and perhaps as many as twenty other women can be identified as the authors of various types of saints' lives through the thirteenth century, the best known of these writers being Hildegard of Bingen. On early women hagiographers see Jane Tibbetts Schulenburg, *Forgetful of Their Sex: Female Sanctity and Society ca. 500–1100* (Chicago and London, 1998), 31–46; Elisabeth Van Houts, "Women and Writing of History in the Early Middle Ages: The Case of Abbess Matilda of Essen and Aethelweard," *Early Medieval History* 1 (1992): 53–68; and Suzanne Fonay Wemple, *Women in Frankish Society: Marriage and the Cloister, 500–900* (Philadelphia, 1981), 181–185.

33. See William MacBain, ed., *The Life of St. Catherine by Clemence of Barking* (Oxford, 1964); Ö. Södergård, ed., *La Vie d'Edouard le Confesseur: Poème anglo-normand du XIIe siècle* (Uppsala, 1948); idem, *La Vie seinte Audrée: Poème anglo-normand du XIIIe siècle*

contemporary biographies, Felipa of Porcellet's *Vida de la benaurada Sancta Doucelina* (Life of the Blessed St. Douceline) has already been mentioned as being composed in approximately 1297. Similarly, Marguerite of Oingt (c. 1240–1310), the prioress of the Carthusian convent of Peloteins, wrote her Francoprovençal *Via seiti Biatrix virgina de Ornaciu* (Life of Béatrix d'Ornacieux) after 1303.[34] The *Life of Isabelle of France* is thus the first life of a woman by a contemporary woman written in the languages of France.[35]

Moreover, the evidence surveyed above indicates a strong likelihood that Agnes of Harcourt is the first woman to have written an extant work of French prose. In addition to the Anglo-Norman hagiographers mentioned above, the *Lais* and *Fables* of Marie de France and the poetry of the *trobairitz* of Provence are well known.[36] But all of these women wrote in verse. The texts of Agnes of Harcourt, Marguerite Porete, Felipa of Porcellet, and Marguerite of Oingt represent the beginnings of female-authored French and Provençal prose.[37] And although claims of absolute priority are always tenuous, Agnes of Harcourt would seem to have written slightly earlier than her three better-known contemporaries.

5. Summary of Contents

The *Letter on Louis IX and Longchamp*

The contents of Agnes's *Letter on Louis IX and Longchamp* have already been summarized in order to demonstrate Agnes's immediate motivations

---

(Uppsala, 1955). The case for Marie de France as the author of the latter work has recently been made by June Hall McCash, "*La Vie seinte Audrée*: A Fourth Text by Marie de France?" *Speculum* 77 (2002): 744–777.

34. See Antonin Duraffour, Pierre Gardette, and Paulette Durdilly, *Les Oeuvres de Marguerite d'Oingt* (Paris, 1965), and Renate Blumenfeld-Kosinski, trans., *The Writings of Margaret of Oingt: Medieval Prioress and Mystic* (Newburyport, MA, 1990).

35. On these female hagiographers see Amy Hollywood, *The Soul as Virgin Wife*, 37–38 and 231 nn. 49–52.

36. Dronke, *Women Writers of the Middle Ages*, 97–106.

37. On the late-twelfth and early-thirteenth-century origins of the first French prose works (presumably) by men see Gabrielle M. Spiegel, *Romancing the Past: The Rise of Vernacular Prose Historiography in Thirteenth-Century France* (Berkeley, CA: 1993), 56–57.

and the *Letter*'s connection with Louis IX's canonization process. The letter is certainly of interest as a new testimony on St. Louis's sanctity and his relationship with women's and Franciscan monasticism. But it is also a crucial source in complementing Agnes's picture of Isabelle in the *Life*, offering unique evidence on the foundation of Isabelle's abbey, her relationship with Louis and his wife, Marguerite, and her death.

The *Life of Isabelle of France*

The *Life* is divided into two sections, following a common hagiographic form; one on Isabelle's life, organized very loosely in chronological fashion, and another on her miracles. There is no further organization into chapters. In its basic outline the text covers much of the biographical ground that one would expect. Agnes begins with a short description of Isabelle's royal parents and their love for their daughter and then gives a brief introductory praise of Isabelle's virtues, noticeably more flowery and metaphorical in tone than the rest of the life. She then moves on to sections on Isabelle's youth, her adult piety, the founding of Longchamp and genesis of its rule, several more anecdotes about her devotion, penitence, and love of silence, and finally a few lines on her last illness and death.

The section on Isabelle's miracles includes several healings that she brought about during her life, then the miraculous signs and events that surrounded her death and translation, and finally a series of cures and other miracles that took place at her tomb. The miracles were experienced by nuns, Franciscans, townspeople from Paris and the surrounding region, and, in perhaps the most notable case, the future Philip IV.

Within this structure, the entire text reads like a loosely organized collection of anecdotes, of collected testimony by nuns (especially Agnes herself), reminiscences by members of the royal family, including Louis IX and his wife, Marguerite of Provence, as well as the recollections of Franciscans and others. This is not the sort of tightly ordered saint's life that moves programmatically from one virtue to another or that seeks to demonstrate a theologically sophisticated progression from one stage of holiness to the next. Agnes employs few metaphors and does not compare her subject with specific earlier saints. There are few explicit biblical quotations in the work, no citations from learned authors, and little evident concern for

specific theological or dogmatic points.[38] Throughout, the emphasis is on recording memories of Isabelle's actions.

In spite of the composite flavor of the text, Agnes does develop several discernible themes in highlighting Isabelle's sanctity. There are her devout personal practices—her routine of daily prayers, her contrition when she was too harsh, her love of silence, and especially her humility. Agnes also underscores Isabelle's adherence to a life of virginity and her ascetic practices, though neither one of these is a major theme in the *Life*. But arguably the most important component of Agnes's picture of Isabelle is her charity—her distribution of food and money to the poor and her desire to help others. Indeed, Agnes portrays her foundation of Longchamp as an extension of this "social conscience." Isabelle wanted to do something useful and pleasing to God and could not decide whether a hospital or a new abbey would be the better idea. She chose the new religious foundation when she was convinced by her confessor, Aymeric of Veire, chancellor of Notre Dame and hence of the university, that a new abbey was more meritorious. Thus Agnes presents Isabelle as first and foremost a saint because of her pious and charitable actions in the world.

Furthermore, it is worth noting that several elements commonly found in *vitae* of medieval holy women are not present in this *Life*. Mysticism, visions, prophecies, and swooning raptures are conspicuous by their complete absence. No mention of Eucharistic piety or concern for souls in Purgatory is found here, and there is comparatively little stress on a particularly bodily piety. Since recent historical scholarship on medieval women tends to emphasize the importance of all of these areas, Agnes of Harcourt's *Life of Isabelle* challenges us to consider whether this rare opportunity to see a medieval female "saint" through the eyes of another woman should spark a reexamination of the nature of women's religious experiences in the thirteenth century.

---

38. Compare Else Marie Wiberg Pedersen's provocative argument that "the texts by and about the religious women of the thirteenth century should be read as theology, as a particular new paradigm for the writing on and transmission of Christian doctrine." Pedersen, "Can God Speak in the Vernacular? On Beatrice of Nazareth's Flemish Exposition of the Love for God," in *The Vernacular Spirit: Essays on Medieval Religious Literature*, ed. Renate Blumenfeld-Kosinski, Duncan Robertsen, and Nancy Bradley Warren (New York, 2002), 185–208, quotation on p. 187.

Agnes's lively, personal narrative also affords us glimpses of Isabelle's intellectual life, her relationship with her family, and her concerns for her abbey. For instance, in describing Isabelle's daily routine of devout prayers and reading, Agnes mentions that in the afternoons Isabelle would study holy writings such as the Bible and saints' lives (*Life*, par. 14). This recollection caused Agnes to remark on how well Isabelle understood Latin. In fact, she had such a command of that language that after her chaplains had written her letters for her, she would have them brought to her so that she could correct any mistakes in the Latin. "And," Agnes assures her readers, "I, Sister Agnes of Harcourt, saw this many times."

Another story related by Agnes gives us some idea of Isabelle and Louis IX's personal relationship as siblings (*Life*, par. 20). King Louis asked his sister for a cap that she had just sewn, but, probably much to his surprise, she refused this royal request, "as I, Sister Agnes of Harcourt, who was present, heard from her mouth with my own ears." Instead Isabelle proposed to donate it to the church, since it was the first one she had ever made. The king then her asked if she would sew another one so that he might have it, to which Isabelle agreed, but only if in fact she should sew another.

Agnes also provides a vivid picture of Isabelle's negotiations with leading Franciscans over the form the rule of her abbey would take (*Life*, par. 23). According to Agnes, Isabelle was very concerned that the rule be good and sure, so she made certain to have it approved by five Franciscan masters of the University of Paris: St. Bonaventure; William of Harcombourg (the minister general and provincial minister for France of the Franciscan order, respectively); her confessor, Eudes of Rosny; William of Meliton; and Geoffrey of Vierson. Isabelle was so involved with the composition of the rule and worked so hard that she was up all night and all day. The Franciscan masters would be present in her chambers to examine everything as it was written, and Isabelle was so intent on making certain that nothing "perilous to souls" should find its way into the rule, and was so anxious that the rule should be approved by the pope, that she could hardly rest.

Episodes such as these give us a picture of Isabelle of France as an educated person who kept careful control over her personal affairs. She appears as a woman who knew her own mind, whether dealing with her chaplains, her royal brother, or a coterie of university intellectuals and church leaders. At the same time, these examples demonstrate Agnes of Harcourt's active role in the text as a first-person voice that frequently acts as the narrative's

authenticating witness and as the authorial presence that lends coherence to her assembled recollections.

In sum, the *Life of Isabelle* is a central text for considering medieval women's lives and vernacular religious literature written by women. In giving us a portrayal of Isabelle of France, Agnes's *Life* offers a new look at key areas of women's religious history—the religious and spiritual goals held by women like Isabelle, the turbulent relationship between women and Franciscans, and the possibilities for women's authority and roles as patrons in the thirteenth century. The testimony by numerous nuns about Isabelle's miracles further offers glimpses of everyday life at Longchamp, revealing the sisters' daily habits, their use of books, and their attempts to attract pilgrims to their founder's tomb.

6. Manuscripts and Previous Editions

The *Life of Isabelle of France*

Agnes's *Life* has up to now only been known in a version edited by the great French scholar Charles du Fresne, better known as Le Sieur du Cange, in 1668.[39] But unfortunately the manuscript from which Du Cange worked has never been recovered, and no others have hitherto been identified. Since the language of Du Cange's version seems to date from rather later than the thirteenth century,[40] and since he was not explicit as to his ex-

---

39. *Histoire de S. Lovys IX du nom Roy de France, écrite par Iean Sire de Ioinville Senéchal de Champagne: Enrichie de nouuelles Obseruations & Dissertations Historiques. Avec les Établissemens de S. Lovys, le Conseil de Pierre de Fontaines, & plusieurs autres Pièces concernant ce regne, tirées des Manuscrits. Par Charles du Fresne, sieur du Cange, Conseiller du Roy, Tresorier de France, & General des Finances en la Generalité de Picardie* (Paris, 1668): 169–181.

40. Paris, "Agnès d'Harcourt, Abbesse de Longchamp," 99: "nous regrettons d'autant plus de n'en avoir pas vu l'ancien manuscrit, que nous avons cru reconnaître, surtout au début du texte de du Cange, plusieurs indices d'altération dans le langage naïf de la religieuse de Longchamp." August Molinier, *Les Sources de l'histoire de France*, vol. 3 (Paris, 1903), 120, no. 2552, describes Du Cange's version as taken from "une copie rajeunie." See the comparison below of passages from Du Cange's text with the present edition.

emplar's provenance or date, there has always been some doubt as to whether his edition preserved Agnes's work in its original form or even contained the complete text.

Thanks to several early-modern witnesses, we know that Agnes's original manuscript remained at Longchamp through the middle of the eighteenth century. Pierre Perrier, a priest associated with the Church of St. Eustache in Paris and author of an unpublished life of Isabelle written for the nuns of Longchamp in 1699, left an engaging preface to this work, which contains a catalogue of the sources he found at Longchamp.[41] First on his list was the original manuscript of Agnes's *Life of Isabelle*. According to Perrier, the manuscript was composed of eight sheets of parchment sewn together into a seven-foot-long roll; the first sheet was written in a hand more recent than the rest, as was a smaller piece added to the second sheet. These were followed by three sheets in the older hand that contained the events of Isabelle's life. Four or five lines in the newer hand were added that described Isabelle's final illness and death. Finally, four more sheets in the original hand contained forty miracles performed by Isabelle in her life and after her death, though two of these miracles were crossed out. In 1741 the Jesuit Stephan Souciet confirmed the basic outline of this description, noting that the thirteenth-century autograph copy of the life was still to be found at Longchamp and that it was in the form of a roll rather than a codex.[42]

---

41. AN L1029, no. 37. Although the author does not give his name, his identity can be firmly established since he mentions having published a *Vie de S. Cloud* in 1696. According to Jacques Lelong, *Bibliothèque Historique de la France*, rev. ed., vol. 2 (Paris, 1769), 659, the author of *La Vie de S. Cloud Prestre, petit fils de Clovis* (Paris, 1696) was "Pierre Perrier, Prêtre (habitué de S. Eustache) né au Village de S. Cloud." The dedicatory letter of this *Vie de S. Cloud* is signed only "P. P." The date of Perrier's life of Isabelle is also revealed by the internal evidence of the preface, since he refers to a decree of Pope Innocent XII "qu'on a fait imprimer l'année passée 1698." Perrier's *Vie de Ste. Isabelle de France* itself exists in a fragmentary state in AN L1029. Another incomplete copy of this life is found in BNF ms. fr. 24950, without the preface. For a transcription of his preface see appendix F in Field, "The Princess, the Abbess, and the Friars."

42. Cited by J. Stilting in his introduction to his Latin translation of Du Cange's edition: "Autographum etiamnum servatur in abbatia Longi-Campi, ubi illud anno 1741 vidit R. P. Stephanus Souciet Societatis nostrae, qui testatur characterem certo esse seculi S. Ludovici, Vitamque scriptam in membrana, non in libeum [*sic*] compacta, sed complicata in volumen." *Acta Sanctorum*, August, 6:787.

There is no reliable indication of the fate of this original manuscript after the revolutionaries turned the nuns out of their abbey and sold off their possessions in 1792. The officials who came to catalogue Longchamp's goods before expelling the nuns left only a cursory assessment of the books they found.[43] Most of the abbey's records, including many accounts on rolls such as the one described above, made their way to the Archives Nationales de France in the course of the nineteenth century. But in spite of misleading claims to the contrary, Agnes's original manuscript of her *Life of Isabelle* has never resurfaced.[44] Certainly no medieval manuscript of Agnes's *Life* is now known to be in the Archives.[45] Thus, although we have

43. AN S4418, "Déclaration et actes Administratifs de 1790": "Dans la salle de la communauté: six corps des bibliothèques contenant mil quatre vingt trois volumes de livres de dévotion, et histoire, parmi lesquells livres de devotion il y a au moins deux cents volumes vieux breviaires et autres de nulle utilité." For an edition of the complete inventory see Duchesne, *Histoire de l'abbaye royale de Longchamp*, 181–183.

44. In an article on the Harcourt family that appeared in 1858, C. Hippeau claimed that Agnes's manuscript could be found in the Archives. *Nouvelle biographie générale*, vol. 23 (Paris, 1858), col. 337. Hippeau says matter-of-factly and without indicating the specific location, "Le manuscrit est conservé aux archives impériales (c'est un rouleau de 8 feuillets de parchemin, cousus à la suite les uns des autres et de sept pieds de long)." This claim seems very unlikely since Paulin Paris attempted without success to trace the whereabouts of this copy for his 1842 article in *Histoire littéraire de la France*. Hippolyte Cocheris's survey of the remnants of Longchamp's archives in 1870 made no mention of this manuscript (*Histoire de la ville et de tout le diocèse de Paris par l'Abbé Lebeuf*. Cocheris's notes and additions, vol. 4, pp. 252–283, survey the holdings from Longchamp at the Archives Nationales), and in 1896 Guy Trouillard declared that no trace of it could be found after a thorough study of the archives. Trouillard, *Etudes sur la discipline et l'état interieur des abbayes de l'ordre des Urbanistes et principalement de l'abbaye de Longchamp du XIIIe siècle au XVIIIe* (thèse de l'École des Chartes, 1896). The original of this thesis is now manuscript F458–459 of the Archives Départementales de Loir-et-Cher. I consulted the handwritten copy held as ms. 1530 by the Bibliothèque Franciscaine Provinciale in Paris. Trouillard discusses the state of the evidence to be found in the Archives Nationales, iii–x, and notes Hippeau's claim on page 26. The wording of Hippeau's description is very close to Perrier's; quite possibly, working from secondhand information, he confused Perrier's description and fragmentary transcription with Agnes's original manuscript. Compare Hippeau's description (cited above) with Perrier's report: "C'est un volume roulé, a l'ancienne manière, composé de huit feuilles de parchemin, cousues bout a bout, long d'environ sept piéds, et large de 8 a 11 pouces sur la longueur."

45. This is despite indications in Duchesne, *Histoire de l'abbaye de Longchamp*, who cites on page 7 n. 1, and again on page 196, "Arch. Nat., L. 1029, Mss de la vie d'Isabelle, par

a fair idea as to the physical characteristics of Agnes's original manuscript and can be certain of its whereabouts until the eighteenth century, it is unlikely that it will reappear.

Fortunately, the story does not end there. Sébastien le Nain de Tillemont, the great seventeenth-century church historian and biographer of Saint Louis, left a sketch for a life of Isabelle, which is today BNF ms. fr. 13753, ff. 89–102.[46] Although the rest of this manuscript was published as part of his *Vie de Saint Louis* in 1847–51,[47] Tillemont's life of Isabelle has remained unedited, perhaps because it is more a series of notes and questions than a finished literary product. In this life, as was his custom, Tillemont included marginal notes when citing his personal manuscripts or printed texts. From these notes it is clear that numbers 60–71 in his notebook B were copies of documents held at Longchamp and that his manuscript B71 was in fact a copy of Agnes's *Life of Isabelle*. In his text Tillemont revealed that this copy was almost entirely in the hand of Antoine Le Maistre.[48]

Agnès d'Harcourt." On page 28 n. 2 he also cites "Arch. Nat., Vie de Madame Isabelle, par soeur Agnès, L. 1021." Clearly, in referring to L1029, he is confusing Perrier's work with Agnes's. The reference to L1021 must simply be an error, since no life of Isabelle is found in that carton. The same year Duchesne's book appeared Ubald d'Alençon verified that no manuscript of Agnes's work was to be found in AN L1029. See "L'Abbaye royale de Longchamp et sa bibliothèque au XVe siècle," *Études franciscaines* 15 (1906): 206–212, verification on p. 208 n. 1. Older references to the contents of AN L1020–1029 can be difficult to track down, since Cocheris's survey makes it clear that the contents of these cartons have been reorganized since 1870. For a summary of their state in that year see Cocheris, *Histoire de la ville et de tout le diocèse de Paris par l'Abbé Lebeuf*, 4:278–279.

46. On Le Nain de Tillemont see Bruno Neveu, *Un Historien à l'école de Port-Royal: Sébastien le Nain de Tillemont (1637–1698)* (The Hague, 1966); Neveu, "Sébastien le Nain de Tillemont, 1637-1698, et l'érudition ecclésiastique de son temps," in *Religion, érudition et critique à la fin du XVIIe siècle et au début du XVIIIe* (Vendôme, 1967), 21–32; and Neveu, "Le Nain de Tillemont et la *Vie de Saint Louis*," in *Septième Centenaire de la mort de Saint Louis: Actes des colloques de Royaumont et de Paris (21–27 mai 1970)* (Paris, 1976), 315–329. The sketch of Isabelle's life was presumably written in the years 1679-1684, when Tillemont was working on his *Vie de Saint Louis*.

47. Jules de Gaulle, ed., *Vie de saint Louis, roi de France, par Le Nain de Tillemont*, 6 vols. (Paris, 1847–1851).

48. BNF ms. fr. 13753, f. 100r. As discussed below, the copy was in fact begun by another hand, but then the bulk of the transcription was carried out by Le Maistre. On Le Maistre see Neveu, *Un Historien à l'école de Port-Royal*, 191–192, and the entry in Louis Moreri, *Le grand dictionnaire historique*, rev. ed. (Paris, 1759).

Although Le Maistre is not a well-studied figure, we know that he was one of Tillemont's instructors at *Les Petites Écoles* of Port Royal in the period around 1646–1655, and had undertaken to compose new lives of the saints "stripped of all fables that less judicious authors have introduced."[49] Presumably he sought out a copy of Agnes's *Life of Isabelle* in this connection, and after his death the manuscript passed directly or indirectly to Tillemont.[50] By rare good fortune, of Tillemont's original notebooks A-F, only B survives and is today BNF ms. fr. 13747. The section on Longchamp forms folios 112r–141v, of which a copy of Agnes's life occupies folios 127r–141v. At the top of folio 127v one reads in the hand of Le Maistre: "La vie de la bienheureuse Isabelle de France soeur du roy S. Loys fondatrice de Longchamp. Copiée tres fidellement sur le manuscrit composé par soeur Agnes de Harcourt, 3ᵉ abbesse de cette maison. C'est un long rouleau de parchemin" (The life of the blessed Isabelle of France, sister of the king Saint Louis, founder of Longchamp. Copied very faithfully from the manuscript composed by Sister Agnes of Harcourt, third abbess of this house. [The manuscript] is a long role of parchment). Clearly he had before him the same manuscript that would be described by Perrier in 1699 and Souciet in 1741. Le Maistre was even kind enough to date the final page of his copy 5 January 1653.

Thus we can identify the copyist of Tillemont's manuscript and its exact date and can state with certainty that it was taken directly from Agnes's now lost original. This hitherto unnoticed copy forms the basis of the present edition of Agnes's *Life of Isabelle*. Though it is not to be expected that even the most scrupulous seventeenth-century transcriber would be able to keep more modern spelling and grammar from creeping into his thirteenth-century text, internal evidence discussed below demonstrates that Le Maistre made a bona fide effort to capture the archaic language of his exemplar.

---

49. Neveu in *Un historien à l'école de Port-Royal*, 191, cites the contemporary witness of Dom Clémencet, found in his *Histoire littéraire de Port-Royal:* "M. Le Maître désiroit depuis de donner les vies des saints purgées de toutes les fables que des auteurs peu judicieux y ont introduites. Il avoit recherché, par le moyen de M. d'Hérouval, son ami, tout ce qu'il avoit pu découvrir d'originaux d'actes des martyrs et de vies édifiantes."
50. Tillemont's notebook B contains dozens of documents in the hand of Le Maistre.

The recovery of a copy unquestionably made from Agnes's original manuscript allows us to attempt to settle the question of the provenance of the manuscript that served as the exemplar for Du Cange's edition of 1668.[51] He informs us that it was provided by Antoine Vyon de Hérouval, a well-known *"erudit"* and *"auditeur des comptes"* in Paris, but does not give any further indications as to its ultimate provenance.[52] It is not even clear whether Hérouval provided him with a medieval manuscript or a more modern copy. Several indications might seem to point to the possibility that Du Cange worked from a seventeenth-century copy of the original manuscript, much as Le Nain de Tillemont did. First, we know that Vyon de Hérouval was an associate not only of Du Cange, but also of Antoine Le Maistre and Le Nain de Tillemont.[53] If Le Maistre was aware of the existence of the original manuscript in 1653, would not his collaborator Hérouval have known of it as well and signaled this fact to Du Cange? Second, this hypothesis might seem to account for the somewhat modernized orthography and morphology of Du Cange's edition, since a copyist working quickly might have introduced modernizations.

On balance, however, the opposite conclusion—that Du Cange's edition was based on another manuscript more distant from the original—carries much more weight. A brief comparison of Du Cange's edition with Le Maistre's transcription serves to demonstrate both that Du Cange's text is fairly distant from thirteenth-century usage and that it is not a thoroughly modernized edition. Compare the following representative passages, drawn from the section of the *Life* that describes Isabelle of France's involvement with Longchamp's foundation and its rule:

---

51. For a brief introduction to Du Cange see Nathan Edelman, *Attitudes of Seventeenth-Century France towards the Middle Ages* (Morningside Heights, NY, 1946), 63–84. For a more detailed, but older, study of Du Cange and his life see Léon Feugère, *Etude sur la vie et les ouvrages de Du Cange* (Paris, 1852).

52. On Vyon d'Hérouval, see Alex. Bruel, "Notes de Vyon d'Hérouval sur les baptisés et les convers et sur les enquêteurs royaux au temps de saint Louis et de ses successeurs," *Bibliothèque de l'École des Chartes* 28 (1867): 610–621; L. Delisle, *Catalogue des Actes de Philippe Auguste* (Paris, 1856), xlvi–xlvii; "Eloge de Monsieur Vion Seigneur d'Herouval, Auditeur des Comptes" in *Le Journal des Scavans* (1689): 226–228; and "Vion (Antoine) seigneur d'Hérouval," in Louis Moreri, *Le Grand dictionnaire historique*, vol. 10 (Paris, 1759), 655.

53. See note 49 above on Le Maistre's collaboration with Hérouval.

Du Cange Edition of 1668 (p. 173)	Le Maistre's Transcription (from paragraphs 22–25 of the present edition)
Li Chancelier Hemery, qui estoit moult preudhomme, & Maistre de Diuinité, qui adonc estoit son Confesseur, li manda que ce n'estoit mie comparaison de l'Hospital, au regard de faire maison de Religion. . . . & tant estoit en grand soing que rien ne passast qui fust perilleux aux ames, si que c'estoit merueille, & de ceste chose elle estoit en si grand soing & en si grand estude, que à peine pouuoit elle reposer, & merueilleusement auoit grand desire que ceste chose fust confirmée du Pape. & sur toutes choses elle vouloit que les seurs de l'Abbaye fussent appellées seurs Mineures, & en nulle maniere la Riule ne luy pouuoit suffire, si ce nom n'y fust mis. . . .	Li chancelers Hemery, qui estoit mout preudome et mestres de divinités, qui adonc estoit son confessor, li manda que ce n'estoit mie comparisson de l'hospital au regart de fere meson de religion. . . . Et tant estoit en grant soin que rien ne passast qui fust p[e]rilleux as ames si que c'estoit mervele. Et de ceste chosce elle estoit en si grant soin et en si grant estoide que a painnes pooit ele repauser. Et mervilleusement eut avoit [sic] grant deisier que ceste chosce fust confermee de l'apoitoile. Et sour toutes chosces elle voloit que les s[e]reurs de s'abeÿe fuissent apelees s[e]reurs meneurs. Et en nulle maniere la riule ne li pooit souffire, se ce nom n'i fust mis. . . .
Elle fut malade de grande maladie auant que la Riule fust confirmée qu'elle estoit aussi comme en langueur de coeur jusques adonc que ceste chose fust accompli par grand sens, & par grande humilité, elle ne vouloit rien requerre à l'Apostole. . . .	Elle fu malade de grans maladies avant que la Riule fust confermee, qu'ele estoit ausi comme en langueur de cuer dusques adonc que cest chosce fu acomplie. Par grand sens et par grant humilitez ele ne voloit riens recreire a l'apotoile. . . .

This comparison demonstrates that Le Maistre's transcription adheres much more closely to thirteenth-century usage than does Du Cange's edition.[54] First, the initial line considered here contains a typical example of Le Maistre's preserving Agnes's use of the Old French two-case declension system, while Du Cange's edition effaces it ("Li Chancelers Hemery . . . mestres" compared to "Li Chancelier Hemery . . . Maistre," where the final "s" signals the masculine nominative singular). Although the declension system was rapidly weakening by the late thirteenth century, numerous dis-

---

54. It should be noted that I have left Du Cange's edition just as it appears while giving Le Maistre's transcription with *u/v* and *i/j* standardized and following modern editorial conventions concerning the additions of accents for Old French.

crepancies between Le Maistre's transcription and Du Cange's edition demonstrate that Agnes's original manuscript still employed it frequently, whereas Du Cange's exemplar had abandoned any attempt at its preservation.[55]

Second, Le Maistre's orthography and morphology are closer to that of the thirteenth century than are Du Cange's. Perhaps the clearest example here is the use of the form "grant" instead of the more modern "grand" and "grande." This discrepancy is consistent throughout the text; athough Le Maistre's transcription does employ the form "grand" six times (including once in the passage cited above) and the form "grandes" once, it uses the form "grant" fifty-six times, and "grans" another ten. It is impossible to be certain whether the occasional appearance of "grand" and "grandes" reflects inconsistent usage by Agnes or slips of Le Maistre's pen, but it is clear that Agnes generally employed the older forms of "grant" and "grans." By contrast, Du Cange's edition always uses the more modern forms, perhaps indicating that his exemplar dated from the fifteenth or early sixteenth century.[56] Similar variations in the example cited above include Le Maistre's reading "sereurs" instead of Du Cange's "seurs"; "pooit" instead of "pouuoit"; and "as" instead of "aux."[57] Moreover, Du Cange's edition sometimes

---

55. It is generally held that in the Île de France the case system was maintained through most of the thirteenth century. See Mildred K. Pope, *From Latin to Modern French with Especial Consideration of Anglo-Norman*, rev. ed. (Manchester, 1952), par. 806. Among clear examples of the telltale use of the masculine nominative singular in "s", compare Le Maistre's readings to Du Cange's: "li peres" for Du Cange's "le pere" (par. 3 and miracle 1); "ycis livres" for "icelui livre" (mir. 15); "li convens" for "li convent" (mirs. 4, 11, 12, 13, 28); "li pos" for "li pot" (mir. 25); "li chiens" for "le chien" (mir. 28); "li brevieres" for "li breviere" (mir. 30); "li enfens" for "li enfant" (mir. 33); "li sercos" for "li sercot" (mir. 35); "li vallés" for "li valet" (mir. 38); "li malades" for "li malade" (mir. 38); "li fix" for "le fils" (mir. 40). The scribe of Du Cange's examplar was evidently confused by the unfamiliar case endings. Hence, where Le Maistre preserves the case system in the masculine plural nominative form "li frere," in Du Cange's edition it becomes the singular "le frere" (mir. 38). Confusion resulting from the presence of the case system may also have resulted in the change in miracle nine from "icis freres" to "le frere Denys."

56. Pope, *From Latin to Modern French*, pars. 773, 780: "These [analogical feminine] forms and others similar were not generalised until Late Middle French." (Indicating the later portion of the Middle French period of approximately 1300–1600.)

57. Le Maistre's transcription reads "as" seven times and "aus" twice; in each place Du Cange has "aux." The form "as" generally gave way to "aus" in the thirteenth century, with "aux" being a later evolution. Pope, *From Latin to Modern French*, par. 843. Le Maistre's

simply replaces archaic terms with more modern words, as in "du Pape" for "de l'Apoitoile." Thus there is no doubt that Le Maistre's transcription brings us closer to Agnes's original text than does Du Cange's edition.

At the same time, Du Cange's edition is certainly not an example of thoroughly modernized seventeenth-century French, suggesting that he or his source had tried to simply change the text to reflect contemporary usage. For instance, consider once more the first line given above; though the traces of the case system are removed, the archaic masculine nominative article "li" remains, though it was no longer used in the seventeenth century.[58] Moreover, although the older term for pope "apostole" was replaced with "pape" in one instance (as noted), in the last line cited above it remains unaltered in the text. If Du Cange or Hérouval had been intent on modernizing a thirteenth-century text, it would have been most odd to have made this emendation in one instance and then left the medieval vocabulary intact only a few lines later. Furthermore, Du Cange included several marginal notes elsewhere in his edition to elucidate obscure words. For instance, on page 171 of his edition he indicates with a marginal note that "heirer" is equivalent to "aller" and on page 173 notes (probably correctly) that "qui" should be read as "li." Clearly, once the text was in Du Cange's hands, he did not attempt to systematically modernize or correct his exemplar.

Since even this brief consideration demonstrates that Du Cange's edition is neither entirely consistent with thirteenth-century nor seventeenth-century usage, the most compelling explanation for this fact would seem to be that Hérouval provided Du Cange with a manuscript produced in the later Middle Ages.[59] Thus Du Cange's edition was based on an exemplar

transcription consistently uses the plural "sereurs," whereas Du Cange's edition reads "soeurs" or (less frequently) "seurs." This change was characteristic of the shift from Old to Middle French after 1300. Ibid., par. 806. The use of the radical "puv" or "pöv" with the verb *poeir* (modern *pouvoir*) was characteristic of Later Middle French. Ibid., par. 955.

58. For further examples of this usage in Du Cange's text see note 55.

59. Although Agnes's *Life of Isabelle* probably did not enjoy a wide medieval circulation, more than one medieval manuscript did exist. The inventories preserved in the Archives Nationales demonstrate that the nuns of Longchamp copied the *Life* into a codex at an early date. Among the items found *"en l'eglise"* in 1325 were *"Item la vie ma dame qui nous funda"* and *"Item livre de la rieule en francois et en Latin et la vie s. clere. Item 1 autre livre ou est la rieule, est en francois et en Latin, et la vie madame,"* AN L1027, no. 5. For an analysis of the Longchamp inventories see Gertrud Mlynarczyk, *Ein Franziskanerinnenkloster im*

at least one step farther removed from the original than Le Maistre's transcription, perhaps resulting in a mélange of late-medieval and early-modern usages.[60]

The *Letter on Louis IX and Longchamp*

Agnes's *Letter on Louis IX and Longchamp* is edited here for the first time from the earliest surviving copy, found in BNF. ms. fr. 11662, ff. 40r–41v. This book began to be copied in the early or mid-fifteenth century, and the section that contains the *Letter* dates from before 1446. The manuscript contains a fifteenth-century calendar (ff. 1–13); a sixteenth-century description of Isabelle's 1521 "beatification" with a translation of the entire 1521 ratification by Cardinal Adrian de Boissy, papal legate to France, of Pope Leo X's bull granting permission to celebrate Isabelle's office at Longchamp (ff. 15–20); a fifteenth-century calendar of anniversaries for the benefactors of the abbey (ff. 22–30);[61] various tables of liturgical usage (ff. 30–37); and a

---

15. Jahrhundert: Edition und Analyse von Besitzinventaren aus der Abtei Longchamp (Bonn, Germany, 1987). These two books reappear in the inventories for 1448, 1467, and 1483, edited by Mlynarczyk (from AN L1028, nos. 5, 7, 9) as "*Item, ii livres de la Ruylle en Latin et en franscois, en l'un y a la Vie madame sainte claire, en l'aultre la Vie madame Isabel, notre sainte mere* (Mlynarczyk, *Ein Franziskanerinnenkloster*, 298, 315, 334). The book containing the rule and the life of St. Clare survives today as AN LL1601, but its twin has been lost. In addition, the first extant inventory of the old royal library of the Louvre, taken in 1373, includes "*La vie suer Ysabeau de Longchamp, qui fu suer S. Loys, et ses miracles.*" There is no trace of this book after the breakup of the royal library in 1435. See Léopold Delisle, *Le Cabinet des manuscrits de la bibliothèque nationale*, vol. 3 (1881; reprint, New York, 1973), 158.

60. In further support of this thesis, it does appear from Du Cange's notes that Hérouval often supplied him with medieval manuscripts which he then copied and returned. In BNF mss. fr. 9496–9500 (Du Cange's "Recueils A–E"), scores of documents from the *chambre des comptes* and monastic cartularies bear marginal notes such as "*communiqué et envoyé par M. de Vyon,*" usually with a date. Since most of these extracts are in Du Cange's hand, it would seem that Hérouval provided original documents that Du Cange would copy as needed and return. We can be certain that Hérouval was not averse to taking possession of manuscripts, since he is known to have "borrowed" two volumes from Royaumont (today BNF mss. lat. 11757 and 11758), which he eventually gave to St.-Germain-des-Prés. See Michel Huglo, "The Dispersal of the Manuscripts of Royaumont in Europe and in North America," *Vincent of Beauvais Newsletter* 25 (2000), 7, 11 n. 13.

61. Edited by Molinier, in *Obituaires de la province de Sens*, vol. 1, pt. 2 (Paris, 1902), 659–664.

fifteenth-century French copy of a bull of exemption granted by Alexander IV on 25 February 1259 (37v–39v).[62] Folios 40r–41v contain the letter given below, with a fifteenth-century preface. After the letter are found a fifteenth-century description of the requirements and procedures for new nuns entering the abbey (41v–43r) and a fifteenth-century Latin copy of a bull from Alexander IV dated 3 March 1259, with the incipit *Devotionis vestre precibus*, allowing the nuns to inherit (43r).[63] The rest of the manuscript (ff. 44–110) is a necrology begun around 1446 and continued up to about 1788.[64]

Although this fifteenth-century copy seems to have introduced modernized orthography and may well have changed, omitted, or added several words, we can be confident that by and large it faithfully preserves Agnes's original letter. Here again Perrier provides decisive evidence that the text in its present form is reliable. First, his initial catalogue of sources includes a description of the original document, allowing us to be certain that it was preserved intact through the seventeenth century.[65] It was a small, approxi-

---

62. A Latin version of this bull is found in AN LL1601 with the incipit *Etsi universe orbis*, edited by F. M. Delorme, "En marge du bullaire Franciscain," *La France Franciscaine*, 3d ser., 21 (1938): 20–22.

63. Edited by Delorme, "En marge," 23.

64. Partially edited by Molinier, *Obituaires de la province de Sens*, vol. 1, pt. 2, 669–683. Folios 44v to 56r date from approximately 1446, since on f. 56r one reads: "Seur Marguerite la Gencienne l'ainsnee a fait escrire le contenu en se volume. Ce fut fait l'an iiiie xlvi que la seur Marguerite avoit vescu religieuse en ceste esglise de Nostre Dame de Longchamp lx et vi ans. [new ink:] et de plus a vescu. 1. an et xxiii iours dieu luy face merce et a tous trespass. Amen."

65. See AN L1029, no. 37: "Un acte, ou atestation, de seur Agnès d'Harcour abbêsse de Lonchamp, touchant ce qui s'est passé dans la fondation de leur Eglise, et dans leur Etablissement. Cet acte est d'une écriture quarrée, belle, et d'une ancre pareille a celle de la vie de la sainte. C'est un morceau de parchemin, de dix pouces et demi de large, sur neuf pouces de haut, d'où pendant aux deux bouts, deux sceaux de cire blanche en ovale, sur lacs de parchemin. Celui qui est a droite, représente l'annonciation de Notre Dame, et S. François au dessous dans une pointe d'arcade, les bras étendus et stigmatises, ces trois figures étant debout. L'ange tient un Rouleau, ou sont ces mots, Ave Maria; et autour du sceau est écrit, Conventus Humilitatis Beatae Mariae. L'autre sceau un peu moins large que le précédent, représente une Religieuse habillée comme à Lon-champ, qui est Sainte Claire, et une autre a genoux, qui semble la prier. Autour est écrit; Sorores Clarissae Humilitatis Beatae Virginis. Cet acte est daté de l'an 1282 le 2 Décembre." It should be noted that Perrier's reading "Clarissae" on the latter seal is highly suspect; the term was never used at Longchamp to my knowledge. It is much more likely that the seal read "Sorores Minores."

mately nine-by-ten-inch piece of parchment, with two seals attached. Second, he included a version of this letter in his own unpublished life of Isabelle of France.[66] Although he introduced updated language and small grammatical changes, the text he produced while citing the original document is for the most part identical to the version found in BNF ms. fr. 11662, indicating that they were both substantially faithful to their lost exemplar.[67]

Furthermore, the copy in BNF ms. fr. 11662 is prefaced by a fifteenth-century paraphrase of the *Letter*'s opening anecdote. This summary attempts to add several details to the *Letter*'s narrative and to offer subtle hints at how Isabelle of France's actions in the *Letter* should be interpreted. These facts are important because they show that the scribe preferred to include this prefatory material rather than to follow the potentially more effective path of silently altering the contents of the *Letter* itself through interpolations or rewritings.[68]

Though the *Letter* has never before appeared in print, Perrier was not the only early-modern author to note the existence of this text in manuscript.

---

66. BNF ms. fr. 24950, 87, 105–106, 139, 169–70. Perrier broke up the letter into chunks and inserted them, with quotation marks, as his narrative demanded.

67. The small, but systematic, modernizations of grammar introduced by Perrier, however, make providing the variants from his copy impractical. And since the copy in BNF ms. fr. 11662 is clearly superior and closer to the original, printing all of Perrier's copy in a parallel column seems unnecessary.

68. This prefatory matter is given here for comparative purposes: "L'eglise des Seurs Mineurs de l'Umilite Nostre Dame de Longchamp pres de Saint Cloud fut faicte et fondee de l'avoir de tres hault et tres noble tres excellente tres humble et tres devote dame, ma dame Ysabel seur monseigneur Saint Loys Roy de France. Et y mist monseigneur Saint Loys la premiere pierre, La Royne Marguerite la second, leur aisné filz la tierce, ma dame Ysabel par humilité la quarte. Et en icelle heur apparurent en la place iii coulons blans et d'une fourme tres gracieux a regarder, et furent ylec bonne piece. Puis s'en volerent si hault vers le ciel qu'ilz ne porent estre veus, et ce virent le roy et la royne, leurs enfans et ma dame Ysabel, et moult de grans gens et d'autres qui y estoient assemblez. Et dirent les plus anciens du pays par leurs sermens que oncques on n'avoit veu couloms blans en ce lieu. Ains on y tuoit les gens et desrobait on marchans, et estoit appelé le lieu de couppe gueule. Et est chose certaine que ma dame Ysabel ot revelation de Dieu que en ce lieu fust faicte ceste abbaye. Et y fut vestu le couvent en la presence des persones dessus nommez, et avecques eulx le ministre de France frere Guillem de Hartembourc. L'an de grace mil. iie et lx, la vegile de Saint Jehan Baptiste qui fut au mercredi. Cy ensuit la teneur de la lettre comment le Roy Saint Loys et ma dame Ysabel sa seur fonderent et commencerent ceste abbaie de Longchamp."

Le Nain de Tillemont possessed a copy, which he referred to as manuscript B62, though it is no longer part of BNF ms. fr. 13747.[69] Sébastien Roulliard also based a section of his seventeenth-century biography on this text.[70] An eighteenth-century description of Longchamp's archives noted its presence and gave a brief, but accurate, summary of its contents.[71] Some of the information contained in Agnes's *Letter* has made its way into biographies of both Isabelle and Louis IX via these indirect paths. For instance, since Le Nain de Tillemont gave all of his notes and documentation to Filleau de La Chaise, the latter's *Vie de Saint Louis* (published in 1688) includes an accurate treatment of this material, citing manuscript B62.[72] Some of the information from the *Letter* was also incorporated into Isabelle's fifteenth-century epitaph, which was then translated into Latin by the Bollandists and so made available to attentive scholars.[73] But by traveling these second-hand routes, the *Letter*'s independent existence has been forgotten and its context obscured.

---

69. Le Comte Riant noticed this lacuna in his "Déposition de Charles d'Anjou pour la Canonisation de Saint Louis," 159 and 159 n. 3. Searching for fragments of St. Louis's canonization process, he noticed Tillemont's reference (*Vie de Saint Louis*, 5:217) to ms. B62, traced it to BNF ms. fr. 13747, but found nothing there. Unfortunately, he made the mistake of looking at page 62, rather than piece no. 62. Discovering that page 62 contained a copy of an altogether different document, he incorrrectly concluded that BNF ms. fr. 13747 was not after all to be identified with Tillemont's manuscript B.

70. Roulliard, *La Saincte Mere,* 192–240.

71. AN L1029, unnumbered document. When I examined this carton in 1999/2000 it contained two unnumbered documents wrapped in pink paper and placed before L1029, no. 1. The first of these is the remains of an eighteenth-century investigation into the papal bulls and privileges held by Longchamp. Several entries have the marginal reading "veu en 1729." The inventory is divided by "armoires." Pages 31–32 list the contents of "un sac dans la 1ere armoir concernant la vocation et beatification de ste. Isabelle." This sack contained, among other documents, the "certification ou lettre d'attestation . . . par soeur Agnes de Harcourt humble abbesse."

72. Filleau de La Chaise, *Vie de Saint Louis,* 2 vols. (Paris, 1688). See 2:375–378, 613–615.

73. This epitaph is now BNF ms. fr. 6214. A Latin translation appeared in *Acta Sanctorum*, August, 6:792–794. The original French text is edited as appendix D in Field, "The Princess, the Abbess, and the Friars."

7. Establishment of the Texts

The manuscript traditions of the two texts edited here are sufficiently different to warrant separate discussions and occasion slightly different editorial policies.[74]

The *Letter on Louis IX and Longchamp*

Since this text exists in a single, clear medieval manuscript (BNF ms. fr. 11662), few editorial changes have been necessary. My edition introduces modern punctuation and capitalization and expands abbreviations in accordance with the spellings that appear elsewhere in the text. Words joined together in the manuscript have been separated in accordance with modern usage (for example "tresreverend" to "tres reverend"). "Ma dame," however, has been left as two words when it appears that way in the manuscript. Orthography follows the fifteenth-century manuscript, except that *i* and *j*, *u* and *v* have been regularized in accordance with modern usage. In adding clarifying diacritical markings, acute accent on stressed final *é* or *és* have been added, as well as the dieresis with forms of "abbaÿe," the verb "oïr," and the name "Loÿs." Quotation marks have been added to signal direct discourse, and paragraph breaks have been introduced editorially. I have left numbers in the form they take in the manuscript, including a period that appears after, but not before, each number.

The *Life of Isabelle of France*

The nature of the base manuscript for this edition presents several challenges. As noted, BNF ms. 13747 is a copy made in January 1653 directly from the original manuscript held at Longchamp. Although most of the manuscript is in the hand of Le Maistre, another hand began the work but left numerous blank spaces where this scribe apparently had difficulty making out the original. This hand continues up to the beginning of paragraph 12 in the present edition. All that can be said about the identity of this copyist is that many other documents in Tillemont's notebooks are in

---

74. In general my editions follow the guidelines established in Alfred Foulet and Mary Blakely Speer, *On Editing Old French Texts* (Lawrence, KS, 1979).

the same hand, but that it is not the hand of Tillemont himself. The transcription was then taken up by Antoine le Maistre, who also added the heading to the first page and went over the initial portion of the text, filling in the blanks left by hand one and making corrections.[75] I have designated these two hands as T1 and T2 (for Tillemont). My edition follows T2 (Antoine Le Maistre) wherever possible. Where Le Maistre made corrections either to T1 or to his own original reading it has been noted in the apparatus. Significant variants found in the 1668 edition of Du Cange (D) are also noted. The recurrent orthographic variations between the base manuscript and Du Cange's edition are not noted, nor are most of the small morphological and syntactical variants.

Two miracles (twenty-six and twenty-seven), which were omitted by Le Maistre, are supplied from Du Cange's edition. This omission is easily explained, since we know from Perrier's description that these two miracles were crossed out in the original manuscript, presumably causing Le Maistre to leave them out of his transcription.[76] They are printed in italics in the present edition. Unfortunately, a noticeable difference in orthography results from this interpolation, which I have not attempted to eradicate. I have, however, removed superfluous diacritical markings, expanded "&" to "et," added quotation marks, standardized *u/v* and *i/j*, and changed capitalization within these two miracles in accordance with the editorial policies used in the rest of the edition.

In addition, for the first four paragraphs of the text we possess a fragmentary transcription that was included by Pierre Perrier in the preface to his 1699 unpublished life of Isabelle of France, preserved in AN L1029, no. 37. This manuscript actually contains fragments of two different, though contemporary, copies of Perrier's preface and transcription, bound together in haphazard fashion out of their original page order. These two hands are designated P1 and P2, with P1 probably representing Perrier's autograph.

---

75. Hand two is identified as Antoine le Maistre, since Tillemont's note in his unpublished Life of Isabelle says that his manuscript of Agnes's *Life* is "presque toute" in his hand. Since the initial section begun by Hand one forms only about one-sixth of the total text, Tillemont's meaning seems clear.

76. AN L1029, no. 37: "Dans le milieu de 7e feuille, il-i-a deux miracles qui sont barrés, ou bâtonnés, de la même ancre . . . ce sont néanmoins deux visions admirables de seur Jeanne de Louvecaines touchant S. Louis et Ste Isabelle."

Parts of the transcription survive only in one or the other of the two hands, and both hands are heavily corrected. Like the base manuscript, this copy was definitely made directly from Agnes of Harcourt's original manuscript held at Longchamp. Thus variants from Perrier's transcription are included as a check on Le Maistre's readings for the opening section of the text. It should be noted that in terms of orthography, Perrier's transcription generally supports Le Maistre's readings against those of Du Cange.

The challenges posed by working with a seventeenth-century copy of the *Life* necessitate an edition that adheres to the base manuscript as closely as possible. No attempt has been made to correct its orthography or to speculate on Agnes's original language. One difficulty concerns the different levels of competence between hand one (T1) and Antoine Le Maistre. It would seem that the former was a less experienced scholar, who found the task beyond him and turned it over to Le Maistre. We therefore have to be aware of differences in conventions and assumptions concerning orthography and morphology between T1 and T2. We can at least, however, be confident that Le Maistre did his best to copy his exemplar letter for letter, since he frequently crossed out readings and replaced them with purely orthographic changes. For example, in the process of checking the work of T1, Le Maistre corrected "chasteté" to "chasteé," "fut" to "fu," "bon" to "boen," "grand" to "grant," and "soeur" to "seur." He applied the same process of orthographic proofreading to his own work, correcting "grande" to "grant," "Evangiles" to "Euvangiles," "salut" to "salu," "secretment" to "secreement," "maison" to "meson," "quelle" to "quele," "peines" to "painnes," "cette" to "cete," "tesmoing" to "tesmong," "yeux" to "eus," "lettre" to "letre," and "Isabel" to "Ysabel," to give only the clearest examples. He was similarly careful in making small corrections that affected grammar and syntax, such as "le" to "li," "prias" to "priat," and "ils" to "il." In each case it is clear that the correction is from an expected seventeenth-century spelling to an orthography more typical of the thirteenth century. Furthermore, at one point Le Maistre copied the phrase "de ses pouvres mains" and noted in parentheses that given the context it should probably have read "de ses propres mains." The fact that he did not silently make this emendation speaks well for the level of his fidelity to his exemplar. Although the number of times Le Maistre had to correct modernisms and errors that had crept into his transcription should remind us that he cannot have amended them all, by the same token they indicate clearly that his intention was to produce an

exact word-for-word and letter-for-letter transcription of Agnes's original manuscript to the best of his ability.

The initial section of the text that was first copied by T1 includes almost no paragraph breaks. I have silently inserted them where they seem necessary. For the rest of the text I have followed paragraph breaks as found in Le Maistre's transcription, with a small number of additional breaks. Text within square brackets represents my rare editorial changes and insertions. Paragraph and miracle numbers have also been added in square brackets. Words have generally been separated following modern usage. The usage of *u* and *v* and *i* and *j* has been modernized where it had not already been done by T1 and Le Maistre. Capitalization and punctuation have likewise been modernized. The base manuscript employs occasional acute-accent, dieresis, and cedilla markings, presumably added to the original text by T1 and Le Maistre. I have added further markings only where necessary for clarity. In a prose work of the late thirteenth century it has not seemed advisable to make extensive use of the dieresis, but it has been employed in particular with forms of "abbaÿe," the verb "oïr," and the name "Loÿs." The cedilla is used in accordance with modern French. I have removed Le Maistre's acute accents over feminine endings of past participles (*ée* or *ées*) in accordance with standard modern editing practices of Old French. Choices in expanding abbreviations are complicated by the lack of uniformity in the base manuscript. Though the text uses both "nostre" and "notre," I have expanded "nre" to "nostre," while leaving "notre" when it is written out that way in the manuscript. Similarly I expand "ste" to "sainte" rather than "saincte" and use "Seigneur" rather than "Segneur," though the alternate forms sometimes appear in the manuscript. Numbers have been left as Roman or Arabic numerals as they appear in the manuscript. Quotation marks have been added to signal direct discourse.

In two instances Le Maistre used the sign "//," perhaps to indicate the end of a sheet of parchment in the original roll. They appear after miracle nine and miracle seventeen. These occurrences are signaled in the notes.

8. Language of the Texts and Translation Principles

It is clear that the fifteenth-century copy of the *Letter on Louis IX and Longchamp* found in BNF ms. fr. 11662 introduces contemporary orthogra-

phy, for instance, "ceulx" in the opening line. Moreover, there is no trace of the Old French two-case declension system preserved in this copy.

On the other hand, the preceding comparison of Du Cange's edition with Le Maistre's transcription has demonstrated that the latter preserves evidence of Agnes's use of the case system. However, this use is hardly consistent. Where more modern forms such as the masculine nominative singular article "le" occur, it is impossible to know whether they accurately reflect Agnes's intentions, but certainly a good deal of variation is to be expected in a work of the late thirteenth century, the very period in which Old French was giving way to Middle French. Among potentially troubling inconsistencies of spelling, the base manuscript sometimes uses the spellings "mai" or "benaite" for "moi" and "benoite."

I have tried to give an English translation that preserves as much as possible the flavor of Agnes's French. For instance, where Agnes employs a single adverb repeatedly, such as "merveilleusement," I generally have maintained the repetitive quality of the text by using the same English word "wonderfully" each time. Similarly, I have let the rather breathless quality of the repeated use of "et" come through by allowing sentences to begin with "and." Agnes's use of pronouns is sometimes ambiguous; for instance, often only the context signals whether "she" refers to one antecedent or another, and in longer sentences pronouns may confusingly shift their referent in midphrase. I have not tried to alter this grammatical ambiguity in my translation. In the *Letter*, I have translated "belle seur" as "good sister" rather than the more literal "sister-in-law," since modern English speakers do not normally address one another as "sister-in-law" in direct conversation. "Sainte" has generally been translated as "holy" where it functions as an adjective modifying another word, like "mère," but simply as "saint" when it appears as a noun. Words within square brackets in the translation are editorial additions. Occasional notes explain my choices in doubtful instances.

9. Reading List

Previous Editions of Agnes of Harcourt's Life of Isabelle of France

Agnes of Harcourt. "La Vie d'Isabelle Soeur de S. Louys, Fondatrice de L'Abbaye de Lonchamp." In *Histoire de S. Lovys IX du nom Roy de France, écrite par Iean Sire de Ioinville Senéchal de Champagne: Enrichie de nouuelles Obseruations & Dis-*

sertations Historiques. Avec les Établissemens de S. Lovys, le Conseil de Pierre de Fontaines, & plusieurs autres Pièces concernant ce regne, tirées des Manuscrits. Par Charles du Fresne, sieur du Cange, Conseiller du Roy, Trésorier de France, & General des Finances en la Generalité de Picardie. Paris: Sébastien Mabre-Cramoisy, 1668: 169–181.

———. "Vita B. Elisabethae seu Isabellae Virginis." In *Acta Sanctorum*, ed. and trans. J. Stilting, 787–809. August, vol. 6. Venice, 1753.

Isabelle of France

Field, Sean. "The Princess, the Abbess, and the Friars: Isabelle of France and the Course of Thirteenth-Century Religious History." Ph.D. diss., Northwestern University, 2002.

———. "New Evidence for the Life of Isabelle of France." *Revue Mabillon*, n.s., 13 (2002): 109–123.

———. "Gilbert of Tournai's Letter to Isabelle of France: An Edition of the Complete Text." Forthcoming in *Mediaeval Studies* 65 (2003).

Garreau, Albert. *Bienheureuse Isabelle de France.* Paris: Éditions Franciscaines, 1943.

———. *Bienheureuse Isabelle de France, Soeur de Saint Louis.* Paris: Éditions Franciscaines, 1955. (A slightly expanded second edition, not labeled as such.)

Jordan, William Chester. "Isabelle of France and Religious Devotion at the Court of Louis IX." Forthcoming in *Capetian Women*, edited by John Carmi Parson's and Kathleen D. Nolan. New York: Palgrave, 2003.

Lynn, Beth, O.S.C. "Clare of Assisi and Isabelle of Longchamp: Further Light on the Early Development of the Franciscan Charism." *Magistra* 3 (1997): 71–98.

Roulliard, Sébastien. *La Saincte Mere, ou Vie de M. Saincte Isabel de France, soeur unique du Roy S. Louis, fondatrice de l'Abbaye de Long-champ.* Paris: Taupinart, 1619.

Worcester, Thomas, S.J. "Neither Married nor Cloistered: Blessed Isabelle in Catholic Reformation France." *Sixteenth Century Journal* 30 (1999): 457–472.

Agnes of Harcourt

De la Roque, Gilles-André. *Histoire généalogique de la maison de Harcourt.* Vols. 2 and 4. Paris: Cramoisy, 1662.

Paris, Paulin. "Agnès d'Harcourt, abbesse de Longchamp." In *Histoire littéraire de la France*, 20: 98–103. 1842. Reprint, Paris: Librairie Universitaire, 1896.

The Abbey of Longchamp

Cocheris, Hippolyte, ed. *Histoire de la ville et de tout le diocèse de Paris par l'Abbé Lebeuf. Nouvelle édition annotée et continuée jusqu'à nos jours par Hippolyte Cocheris.* Vol. 4. Paris, 1870.

Duchesne, Gaston. *Histoire de l'abbaye royale de Longchamp (1255 à 1789).* 2d ed. Paris: Daragon, 1906.

Field, Sean. "The Abbesses of Longchamp up to the Black Death." Forthcoming in *Archivum Franciscanum Historicum* 96 (2003).

Gallia Christiana. Opera et studio monachorum congregationis S. Mauri ordinis S. Benedicti. Vol. 7. Paris, 1744.

Mlynarczyk, Gertrud. *Ein Franziskanerinnenkloster im 15. Jahrhundert: Edition und Analyse von Besitzinventaren aus der Abtei Longchamp.* Bonn, Germany: Röhrscheid, 1987.

Molinier, Auguste L., ed. *Obituaires de la Province de Sens.* Diocèse de Sens et de Paris. Vol. 1. Pt. 2. Paris: Imprimerie Nationale, 1902.

Louis IX of France

Carolus-Barré, L. *Le Procès de canonization de Saint Louis.* Rome: École Française de Rome, 1994.

Jordan, William Chester. *Louis IX and the Challenge of the Crusade.* Princeton: Princeton University Press, 1979.

Le Goff, Jacques. *Saint Louis.* Paris: Gallimard, 1996.

Richard, Jean. *Saint Louis: Crusader King of France.* Edited by Simon Lloyd. Translated by Jean Birrell. Cambridge: Cambridge University Press, 1992.

Tillemont, Sébastien le Nain de. *Vie de saint Louis, roi de France.* Edited by J. de Gaulle. 6 vols. Paris: Renouard, 1847–1851.

LETTER ON
LOUIS IX
AND
LONGCHAMP

Edition

[1] A tous ceulx qui ces presentes lettres verront, seur Agnes de Hare-court humble abbesse des seurs mineurs encloses en l'Abbaÿe de l'Umilité Nostre Dame de Longchamp¹ et tout le couvent de ce mesmes lieu, // (f. 40v) salut en Nostre Seigneur.

[2] Nous faisons assavoir a tous ceulx qui ces lettres verront que nostre tres reverend et saint pere monseigneur le roy Loÿs fonda nostre eglise et mist de sa propre main la premiere pierre ou fundement. Et ma dame la royne Marguerite sa femme y mist la seconde pierre, et monseigneur Loÿs leur ainsné filz y mist la tierce pierre. Et ma dame Ysabel sa bonne seur, nostre saincte mere, y mist la quarte pierre. Et en icelle heure que ilz faisoient ceste chose, iiij. coulons blans s'assirent en ce lieu. Et si tost comme ma dame la royne Marguerite les vit, elle dist a ma dame Ysabel la seur le roy, "Regardez belle seur! Vecy iiij. coulons blans, qui monstrent que la Saincte Trinité soit au commencement de nostre oeuvre." Je seur Agnes de Harecourt, je seur Ysabel de Rains, je seur Angre, je seur Julienne, je seur Mahault de Gon-darville, et plusieurs autres seurs oÿmes ces choses de la bouche ma dame la royne Marguerite dessus dicte qui les nous raconta en verité, si comme celle qui y avoit esté presente en sa propre personne.

[3] Icellui nostre tres reverend et saint pere monseigneur le roy Loÿs fut present moult devotement quant nous entrasmes en la religion et nous encloist. Et assez tost aprez il entra par devers nous, si comme il y pouoit entrer parmy nostre ruyle par le congié de monseigneur le pape. Et ma dame Ysabel sa bonne seur, nostre saincte mere, fut en sa compaignie. Nous fusmes ensemble devant lui en chapitre. Il se assit aussi bas comme nous, et nous fist le premier sermon et enseignement que nous eussions eu puis que nous y estions // (f. 41r) entrees, et disoit que nous devions prendre ex-emple a monseigneur saint François et a ma dame saincte Clere et aux aul-tres sains qui vesquirent si sainctement et si parfaictement, et que nous

Translation

To all who will see the present letter, Sister Agnes of Harcourt, humble abbess of the Enclosed Sisters Minor of the Abbey of the Humility of Our Lady of Longchamp, and the whole convent of this same place, greetings in our Lord.

We make known to all who will see this letter that our very reverend and holy father, Monseigneur the king Louis, founded our church and with his own hand placed its first stone at the foundation. And Madame the queen Marguerite, his wife, placed the second stone, and Monseigneur Louis, their oldest son, the third. And Madame Isabelle, his good sister, our holy mother, placed the fourth stone. And at the very moment they were doing this, three white doves perched there. And as soon as Madame the queen Marguerite saw them, she said to Madame Isabelle, the king's sister, "Look, good sister! Here are three white doves, who show that the Holy Trinity is present at the beginning of our work." I, Sister Agnes of Harcourt, I, Sister Isabelle of Reims, I, Sister Angre, I, Sister Julienne, I, Sister Mahaut of Gondarville, and many other sisters heard these things from the mouth of Madame the queen Marguerite, mentioned above, who recounted them to us in truth, as one who had been present there herself.

Our same very reverend and holy father, Monseigneur the king Louis, was most devoutly present when we entered into religion and enclosed us. And soon after, he entered among us, as he could enter there according to our rule by permission of Monseigneur the pope. And Madame Isabelle, his good sister, our holy mother, accompanied him. We were gathered together before him in chapter. He seated himself right down on our level, and he gave the first sermon and teaching that we had had since we had entered there, and he said that we ought to take as our example Monseigneur Saint Francis and Madame Saint Clare and other saints who lived with such sanctity and perfection, and that we should begin so high

devions commencier si hault que les autres qui vendroient aprés nous n'y
peussent attaindre, et que nous devions estre mirouer a toutes les autres
femmes de religion et mener telle vie que les autres y peussent prendre
bon exemple. Et adonc et autres fois il nous dist moult de bonnes paroles qui
longues seroient a raconter.

[4] Et quant il entroit par devers nous, devotement et humblement aloit
visiter les malades, et aloit veoir humblement que le couvent devoit mengier. Et quant ma dame Ysabel sa bonne seur fut trespassee, il mesmes en
sa propre personne garda la porte de nostre enclos pour ce que nulx n'y en-
trast qui n'y deut entrer. Et quant il vit le corps de ma dame sa seur en nostre
eglise, vestu de nostre habit, il s'agellougna et inclina parfondement en signe
de grant devocion, et aprés il nous conforta moult doulcement et moult
charitablement. Et quant il deut aler oultre mer, il entra devers nous en
chapitre et s'agellougna moult humblement et moult devotement en requer-
ant aide d'oroisons. Et plusieurs de nous tenons fermement qu'il nous a
garies de fievres et d'autres grans maladies.

[5] Il donna a nostre eglise grant quantité de la vraye crois en ung vaissel
d'or, et une des espines de la saincte couronne en ung vaissel d'argent et de
cristal. Il donna tout le merrien de nostre eglise et les estaus du monstier. Il
donna les quins et les admortissemens de noz //(f. 41v) rentes et vj.ˣˣ livres
parisis pour faire noz despens quant nous y entrasmes nouvellement, et lx.
livres de bois en la forest de Compiegne. Et tant comme il vesqui il nous
donna nostre ardoir au bois d'emprés nous, et moult d'autres chose qui
longue chose seroit a raconter.

[6] Et en tesmoing de toutes ces choses qui sont vraies si comme nous les
avons veues et oÿes, nous avons mis noz seaulx en ces presentes lettres. En
l'an de l'incarnation Nostre Seigneur mil. iie. iiii.ˣˣ et ii. en la ii.e nonne du
mois de Decembre.

that the others who would come after us would not be able to equal us, and that we should be a mirror to all the other women of religion and lead such a life that the others could take it as a good example. And then and at other times he said many good words to us that would be lengthy to recount.

And when he would enter among us, he would devoutly and humbly go to visit the sick and go humbly to see what the convent had to eat. And when Madame Isabelle, his good sister, passed away, he himself in his own person guarded the door of our enclosure so that no one entered there who should not enter. And when he saw the body of Madame his sister in our church, dressed in our habit, he kneeled and bowed deeply as a sign of great devotion, and afterward he comforted us very sweetly and charitably. And when he had to go overseas, he entered among us in our chapter and kneeled very humbly and very devoutly, asking for the aid of prayers. And many of us firmly believe that he cured us of fevers and other great maladies.

He gave to our church a great quantity of the true cross in a golden vessel, and one of the thorns from the holy crown in a vessel of silver and crystal. He gave all the building materials for our abbey and the stalls of the church. He gave [us] the tax of a fifth and the amortisation[1] of our rents and 120 Parisian livres for our expenses when we first entered here and 60 livres of wood in the forest of Compiègne. And as long as he lived he gave us our firewood from the woods around us and many other things that it would be a lengthy affair to recount.

And in witness of all these things, which are true just as we have seen and heard them, we have affixed our seals to the present letter, in the year of the incarnation of our Lord one thousand two hundred and eighty-two, on the second day before the nones of the month of December [4 December 1282].

Notes

Note to Edition

1. The words "de Longchamp" were not included in Pierre Perrier's 1699 transcription of this letter, made directly from the original document (see introduction), and thus may be a fifteenth-century addition. The beginning of Perrier's version (with obviously updated language) is included here from BNF ms. fr. 24950, p. 87, for comparison:

"A tous ceux qui ces presente lettres verront, seur Agnes d'Harcourt humble abbesse des seurs mineurs encloses en l'Abbaÿe de l'Humilité Nostre Dame et tout le convent de ce meme lieu, salut en Nostre Seigneur. Nous fesons savoir a tous ceux qui ces lettres verront que nostre tres reverent et saint pere monseigneur le roi Louis fonda nostre eglise, et mit de sa propre main la premiere pierre au fondement; que madame la reine Margueritte sa femme i mit la seconde pierre; que monseigneur Louis leur fils ainé i mit la troisiesme pierre; et que madame Isabelle sa bonne seur nostre sainte mere i mit la quatriesme pierre, que lors qu'ils fesoient cela, trois pigeons blans vinrent s'abbattre en ce lieu, et qu'ausi tost que madame la reine Margueritte les vit, elle dit a madame Isabelle seur du roi: Regardez belle soeur, voici trois pigeons blans qui montent que la Sainte Trinité est au commencement de nostre euvre; je seur Agnes d'Harcourt; je seur Isabelle de Rheims; je seur Angre; je seur Julienne; je seur Mahaut de Godarville, et plusieurs autres seurs ouîmes ces choses de la bouche de madame la reine Marguerite susdite qui nous les raconta en verité comme celle qui i avoit été presente en sa propre personne."

Note to Translation

1. This legal term, preserved in the English word "mortmain," refers to land granted to a monastery or church in perpetuity, emphasizing "the future and permanent inalienability of the property conveyed and the peculiar nature of the church as possessor." See William Chester Jordan, "Mortmain," in *Dictionary of the Middle Ages*, vol. 8 (New York, 1987): 488–489.

LIFE OF ISABELLE OF FRANCE

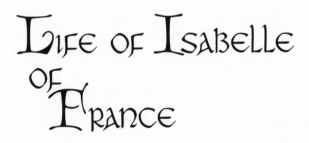

Edition

La vie de la bienheureuse Isabelle de France soeur du roy S. Loys fondatrice de Longchamp. Copiée tres fidellement sur le manuscrit composé par soeur Agnes de Harcourt, 3ᵉ abbesse de cette maison. C'est un long rouleau de parchemin.[1]

[1] Nous avons proposé d'escrire la vie de nostre saincte et benoite dame et mere madame Yzabeau de France, a la requeste de monseigneur le roy de Cecile son frere germain, selonc ce que Diex nous donrra sa grace, a l'onneur de Nostre Seigneur Jesu Crist et de ceste benoite saincte et a l'edification de[2]
5   sainte[3] eglise.

[2] Et[4] premierement nous dirons qui elle fu, et de quex gens estraite, et aprés[5] dirons de s'enfance et de sa conversation, quelle vie elle mena.

[3] Nostre[6] saincte mere et dame madame Ysabeau fut estraicte de royal ligniee, et fu fille du tres noble roy Loÿs de France qui fu filz du roy Phe-
10   lippe, et fu fille de la tres noble royne de France madame la royne Blanche qui fu fille au roy d'Espaigne. Li peres et la mere n'avoient plus de filles et merveilleusement l'amoient et avoient chiere, et la tenoit l'en a la plus noble dame qui fust en terre.[7]

[4] En sa jouenece elle estoit moult gracieuse et de grant beauté, et ja soit
15   ce qu'elle fust si noble de lignage, encore fu elle plus haute et plus noble de moeurs. //(f. 127r). Elle savoit bien que icelle seule est la vraye[8] noblece qui est ornement de l'ame par bonté de l'ame et par saincte vie[9] si comme[10] apparra cy aprés. Elle fu fille et espouse et especial amie de Nostre Seigneur Jesu Crist, et touz ses desiriers et toute s'entention et tous ses labours si
20   furent de destruire pechiez et de planter vertus en soy, et en autrui. Elle fu mirouoir d'innocence, exemplaire de penance,[11] rose de patience, lis de

Translation

The life of the blessed Isabelle of France, sister of the king Saint Louis, founder of Longchamp. Copied very faithfully from the manuscript composed by Sister Agnes of Harcourt, third abbess of this house. [The manuscript] is a long role of parchment.

We have proposed to write the life of our holy and blessed lady and mother, Madame Isabelle of France, at the request of Monseigneur the king of Sicily, her full brother, in so far as God will grant us his grace, for the honor of our Lord Jesus Christ and of this blessed saint and for the edification of the holy church.

And first we will tell who she was, and of her lineage, and then we will tell of her childhood and of her conversation [and] what sort of life she led.

Our holy mother and lady, Madame Isabelle, was of royal lineage and was the daughter of the very noble king Louis of France, who was the son of King Philip, and the daughter of the very noble queen of France, Madame the queen Blanche, who was the daughter of the king of Spain. Her father and her mother had no other daughters, and they loved her wonderfully and held her dear, and she was held to be the most noble lady in the world.

In her childhood she was graceful and of great beauty, and even though she was so noble in lineage, she was even higher and more noble in morals. She well understood that the only true nobility is that which is an ornament of the soul through goodness of the soul and through a holy life, as will appear hereafter. She was the daughter and wife and special friend of our Lord Jesus Christ, and all her desires and all her intention and all her labors were to destroy sin and to plant virtue in herself and in others. She was a mirror of innocence, an example of penance, a rose of patience, a lily

chasteé,[12] fontaine de misericorde. Elle fu[13] escolle de toutes bonnes moeurs, quar elle fu escolié especial[14] de l'escole de Nostre Seigneur Jesu Crist, qui dist a ses disciples, "Apprenez[15] de moi que je sui doux et deboenneres et humbles de quer." Cette[16] leçon retint bien especialement notre benoite et sainte et noble dame et mere madame Issabel,[17] quar en toutes ses heuvres[18] n'apparoit fors humilité de quer et debonnereté, selon ce[19] que Salemon ensenge: "Tant comme tu es plus grans, humilie toi en tes[20] heuvres et en toutes choses."[21]

[5] Et[22] cette benoite et excellante dame en sa jeunece tres voulentiers[23] demouroit en la chambre et apprenoit a entendre la devine escriture et ne vouloit aler es esbatements la ou les fames de ses freres et les autres dames aloient, et quant elle fut entroduite des letres //(f. 128r) soufisamment, elle s'ettudiet a aprendre a ouvrer de saie et fesoit estoles et autres paremens a sainte eglise, et quant en li aportoit images de Notre Segneur ou de Notre Dame, ele les recevoit si joieusement que ce estoit merveilles et montroit bien qu'ele les amat miex et avoit plus chiers que nul autre present d'aournement que l'en li [peut faire].[24]

[6] [A]u tans[25] de sa jeunece quant madame la raine Blanche sa mere vivoit, qui merveilleusement l'amoit tendrement et fesoit aourner son cors de mout biaus et haults[26] aournemens et de riches, ele me dit de sa bouche qu'ele avoit ausi boen quer et ausi devot a Notre Segneur quant ele avoit ces riches aournements en son chief et en son quors comme elle avoit quant ele ot abit plus religieus. Et croi qu'il en i auvra des autres qui bien le temoin- gneront se besoing en est. Et cette chose montrait bien que son quer estoit tousjours bien ententif a amer Nostre Segneur et que l'amour de son quer n'estoit pas aux aournements ne a la gloire de cett chetif monde.

[7] Elle fu juree[27] de ses amis a prendre a mariage au fiux de l'empereur de Romme qui devoit estre her[28] de l'Empire, mes onques au mariage cor- porel ne s'en vout[29] asentir, quar elle avoit eslu le pardurable espoux Nostre Segneur Jesu Crist en parfaite virginité.[30] //(f. 128v) Monsegneur la ppape[31] Inocent quart li escrit et la preecha merveilleusement a[32] li[33] marier pour les pourfis[34] qui viennet[35] du mariage de tiex[36] dame. Nous en avons enquore les letres en notre abaïe. Et aprés ce[37] qu'il vit qu'il ne pouoit son boen propos muer, il li[38] escrit unes autres letres esquelles[39] il s'eforçoit quan qu'il pouoit a[40] li louer son boen[41] propos et l'ettat de virginité, et ces letres meismes avons nous en notre abaïe.

of chastity, a fountain of mercy. She was a school of all good morals, because she was a special student of the school of our Lord Jesus Christ, who said to his disciples, "Learn from me for I am gentle and good-natured and humble of heart."[1] Our blessed and holy and noble lady and mother, Madame Isabelle, retained this lesson especially well, because in all her works appeared only humility of heart and gentleness, in keeping with what Solomon teaches: "The greater you are, the more humble yourself in your works and in all things."[2]

And this blessed and excellent lady in her childhood very willingly stayed in her chamber and learned to understand divine Scripture and did not want to go to the entertainments where the wives of her brothers and the other ladies went, and when she was instructed sufficiently in her letters, she would study to learn how to work with silk and would make stoles and other apparel for the holy church. And when she was brought images of our Lord or of our Lady, she would receive them so joyously that it was wonderful and would clearly demonstrate that she loved them more and held them more dear than any other present or ornament that one could give her.

In the time of her childhood, when Madame the queen Blanche, her mother, was alive, who loved her wonderfully and tenderly and caused her body to be adorned with many beautiful and high and rich ornaments, she told me with her own mouth that she had just as good a heart and was just as devoted to our Lord when she had these rich ornaments on her head and on her body as she had when she had more religious attire. And I believe that there will be others who will certainly testify to this if need be, and this matter certainly showed that her heart was always intent on loving our Lord and that the love of her heart was not for ornaments nor for the glory of this wretched world.

She was pledged by her family[3] to contract a marriage with the son of the emperor of Rome, who was to be the heir to the empire, but she never wanted to assent to corporal marriage, because she had chosen the enduring husband, our Lord Jesus Christ, in perfect virginity. Monseigneur the pope Innocent IV wrote to her and preached wonderfully to her to marry for the benefits that would come from the marriage of such a lady. We still have this letter in our abbey. And after he saw that he could not alter her good purpose, he wrote another letter to her in which he set himself as much as he could to praise her good purpose and the state of virginity, and this same letter we [also] have in our abbey.

[8]   Ele avoit trop durement biau chief et reluisant pour neant fut ce, et quant l'en li pignoit ses damoiseles prenaient ses[42] cheveus qui li cheaient et les gardaient mout soigneusement, si que un jour elle leur demanda pourquoy elles fesaient ce, et elles respondirent, "Dame,[43] nous les gardons pour ce que quant vous serez sainte[44] nous les garderons comme reliques." Elle s'en riait et tournoit tout au neant et tenoit a folie ces chosses. Je suer Agnes de Harecourt oï[45] ces chosses de la bouche a ses damoiselles qui li servoient, et encore é je[46] de ses cheveus de sa jeunece.

[9]   Il avint que en sa jeunece une trop grant maladie d'agüe[47] la prit, et au commencement de la maladie il convint[48] madame la raine Blanche sa mere aler loint une journee ou .ii. pour les //(f. 129r) besoingnes du reaume, et la lesa a Seint Germain en Laie et madame la raine Marguerite avec li. Et tantot la maladie agrega si forment que l'on n'i atendoit ausi comme point de vie, et envoia l'en[49] quere madame sa mere et monseigneur le roi[50] son frere en grant hate. Et quant elle vint la, elle la trouva mout malade et en peril de mourir, de quoi elle fu mout atteinte de mesese de son quer comme mere. Elle envoya soingneusement par tout pour requiere oraisons et especiaument en Ananterre,[51] mesmement a une personne mout religieuse et moult contemplatisve a qui elle monstroit moult a certes[52] la mesese de son quer pour ce que celle persone contrainsit[53] plus atteingnantivement[54] Nostre Segneur par oraison pour aider[55] sa fille. Et celle personne li manda par escrit que sa fille respasseroit de cette maladie, mes fut elle certeine que jamés son quer ne seroit[56] au monde ne aus chosses du monde, et il i parut bien quar onque puis elle ne mit sus son quors nul de ces riches aournements, mes de jour en jour et de plus en plus elle se donnoit du tout a oraison et a heuvres de perfection et en vie religieuse. Et de robes et de lieure et de toutes les chosses qu'il li convenoit //(f. 129v) a son quors aourner, elle despisoit[57] toutes richesses corporelles pour acquere[58] a l'ame de li[59] aournements de vertu et de humilité.

[10]   Ceste benoite et excellente dame avoit si grant[60] amour a pureté et a innocence des s'enfance que a paines le porroit on raconter, si comme l'en le poit apertement[61] cognoistre en toutes ses oevres. Elle ne poit souffrir que l'en dist nul mal d'autruy devant li ne nulle meçoingne, et en avoit si grand horreur que toute la face l'en muoit,[62] si qu'il avenit[63] aucune fais[64] que quant aucunes personnes venoient a li pour[65] demander l'aumosne ou pour aucunes besoingnes elle envoyoit a eux avant qu'ilz veinssent devant li, et leur fesait dire qu'il se preinssent bien garde qu'il ne deissent fors que verité, et que s'ele

She had a very beautiful head of hair, almost lustrous, and when it was combed, her damsels would gather her hairs that would fall and would keep them very carefully, so that one day she asked them why they did this, and they responded, "Lady, we are keeping them so that when you are a saint we will keep them as relics." She laughed at this and turned it all to nothing and held these things to be folly. I, Sister Agnes of Harcourt, heard these things from the mouth of the damsels who served her, and I still have some of her hairs from her youth.

It happened that in her childhood she was taken very sick with the ague, and at the beginning of the malady it was necessary for Madame the queen Blanche, her mother, to go away for a day or two for the affairs of the realm, and she left her at Saint-Germain-en-Laye and Madame the queen Marguerite with her. And shortly the malady worsened so acutely that she was thought to be at the point of death, and Madame her mother and Monseigneur the king, her brother, were sent for in great haste, and when she arrived she found her very sick and in peril of death, by which she was much afflicted in her heart as a mother. She carefully sent everywhere to ask for prayers, and especially to Nanterre,[4] to a very religious and contemplative person, to whom she indeed revealed the affliction of her heart so that this person with her prayers would more attentively compel our Lord to aid her daughter. And this person informed her by writing that her daughter would recover from this malady, but she was certain that her heart would never be in the world, nor in the things of the world. And this certainly came to pass, because nevermore did she put on her body any of those rich adornments, but from day to day and more and more she gave herself entirely to prayer and to works of perfection and to a religious life. And as for robes and ribbons and all the things that were suitable for her to adorn her body with, she despised all corporeal riches in order to acquire for the soul the adornments of virtue and humility.

This blessed and excellent lady had such a great love of purity and innocence ever since her childhood that it can hardly be recounted, as could clearly be recognized in all her works. She could not stand that any evil should be said of another in her presence, nor any lie, and she had such a great horror of this that her whole face would be contorted, so that it happened sometimes that when people came to her to ask for alms or for other needs, she would send to them before they had come before her and have it said to them that they should take care that they not speak anything but the

95 apercevoit qu'il deissent verité ele feroit plus volentiers ce que il li recroient.[66] Je seur[67] Agnes[68] de Harecourt porte tesmoingnage de cette chose
qui aucune fois fiz ce message.

[11]   Et en s'enfance elle estoit si accoustumee a oraison que veiz dessoubz la couverture de son[69] lict estait[70] elle en oroison a coutes et a genouz
100 et se reponnoit[71] dessoubz sa couverture, si qu'il avint un[72] matin qu'il de-
voient //(f. 130r) hier que cis qui devoit trousser et emmaler[73] les lictz et
les raubes embraça le couvertoir et la raube qu'il cuidoit que la robe fust ensi
entortillee dedenz le lit, et c'estoit nostre benoite dame et sainte mere madame Yzabel qui estoit ylesques[74] a coutes et a genouz en oroison. Et quant
105 il vaut prendre la raube ele s'escria[75] si haut que les dames i acoururent[76]
et celi fu touz esbahiz et espaventés. Je seur Agnez de Harecourt oï ceste
chose de la bouche mon seigneur le sainct roy Loïz[77] qui le nous raconta,
et Mehaus[78] de Godarville qui fu en son service oï cette mesme chose
de la bouche madame Helins de Buesemont qui avoit esté avec madame des
110 s'enfance.

[12]   Icele mesme[79] madame Helins[80] disoit que elle avoit veu tans[81]
19 ans que cette benoite dame ne maiga onques son sol de pain. Et icelle
madame[82] Helins recordoit que madame la reine Blanche sa mere li disoit
que s'elle maigoit un seul morsel ele donrroit quarente sous aux pouvres et
115 ausi pour parler une seule parole a monseigneur le roi son frere ele li
proumetoit aucune fois 40 sous a donner as pouvres, et mout de fois ele ne[83]
le voloit pas fere pour choscе qu'ele proumeist pour l'amour qu'ele avoit a
astinence et a silence.

[13]   En sa joinece ele geunoit[84] trois jours en la semaine et quant ve-
120 noit a l'eure du maichier,[85] ele maigoit si tres petit que nul cors humain n'en
peut estre soutenus se //(f. 130v) la grace de Dieu ne le feist.[86] Et souventefois quant ele avoit tout jour geuné, sa viande estoit un peu de pouree et de
pois baiens. Ele estoit servie d'assés de mes et de bons viandes, si comme il
affroit a tel dame, et tout envoiet[87] a l'aumosne et es enfermeries des gens de
125 religion, et du pire ele maingoit et tres petit, et a chacun morsel qu'ele maingoit ele en metoit dix a l'aumone[88] pour Diu et pre[s]que tout son maingier
ele estoit en oroison et en silence. Ele seoit mervilleusement[89] petit a la
table, si que souvent ele se levoit avant que ses fames qui la servoient et ren-
doit graces si tres devotement et si ententivement que c'estoit mervele. Ele
130 faisoit dire le devin office mout deligamment et l'escoutoit tout mout[90] devotement et mout ententivement.

truth and that if she saw that they spoke the truth she would do more willingly that which they requested of her. I, Sister Agnes of Harcourt, who sometimes carried this message, bear witness to this matter.

And in her childhood she was so accustomed to prayer that sometimes she would be under the blankets of her bed in prayer, resting on her elbows and on her knees, and would hide herself under her blanket, so that it happened one morning when they had to depart that the man who had to pack up and put away the beds and the bedclothes took the blanket and the bedclothes, and he thought that the bedclothes were all twisted up in the bed, and it was our blessed lady and holy mother, Madame Isabelle, who was there on her elbows and on her knees in prayer. And when he wanted to take the bedclothes, she cried out so loudly that the damsels came running and he was quite frightened and astonished. I, Sister Agnes of Harcourt, heard this from the mouth of Monseigneur the holy king Louis, who recounted it to us, and Mehaut of Gondarville, who was in her service, heard this same thing from the mouth of Madame Helen of Buesemont, who was with Madame from her childhood.

This same Madame Helen would say that she had seen for nineteen years that this blessed lady never ate her portion of bread. And this same Madame Helen would relate that Madame the queen Blanche, her mother, would tell her that if she ate a single morsel, she would give forty sous to the poor, and also if she would speak a single word to Monseigneur the king, her brother, she would promise her sometimes forty sous to give to the poor, and many times she did not want to do it because of something she had promised out of the love that she had of abstinence and of silence.

In her childhood she would fast three days a week, and when the hour of mealtime would arrive, she would eat so little that no human body could be sustained by it if the grace of God did not bring it about. And often when she had fasted all day her nourishment would be a bit of vegetable soup and split peas. She would be served plenty of dishes and good food just as was befitting to such a lady, and she would send it all for alms and for the infirmaries of the religious, and she would eat from the worst, and very little. And for each morsel that she would eat she would put aside ten as alms for God, and through almost all her mealtime she would be in prayer and in silence. She spent wonderfully little time at table, so that often she would get up before her women who served her and would give thanks so very devotedly and attentively that it was wonderful. She would have the Divine Office said most diligently and would listen to it most devoutly and attentively.

[14] Ele se levoit pour dire ses matines grant piece devant le jour et ne se recouchoioit point et estoit continuement en oroison jusques a haut midy. Et souventefois ele faisoit ceux qui la servoient maingier avant que li, pour estre plus longuement en oroisons. Ele ne parloit point quant ele dissoit ses heures, ne devant prime, ne puis qu'ele avoit dit complie s'ele n'estoit malade. Ele estoit mervileusement en oroisons en quaresme, plus qu'en autre tans, et estoit souvent en grant[91] abondance de larmes, si que quant ele issoit de son oratoire, ele avoit les yeus si enflez et si rouges qu'il aparoit bien que mervilleusement avoit espandues de larmes. Ele avoit acoutumé a estre en //(f. 131r) oroison en son oratoire jusques a l'eur de haut midy et adunc ele yssoit de son oratoire et entroit en sa chambre et illec estoit juques a nonne en estude des saintes escritures, si comme de la Bible et des saintes Euvangiles[92] et des autres vies des sains. Car ele entendoit mout bien latin et si bien l'entendoit que quant ses chapelains li avoient escrites ses letres qu'ele fesoit faire en latin et ils li aportoient, ele les amendoit quant il y avoit aucun fau mot. Et je seur Agnes de Harecourt vi ceste chosce pluiseurs fois et autres persones ausi. Mervilleusement oïet[93] la parole Nostre Seigneur et souvent la fesoit dire devant li.

[15] Ele estoit de mout tendre conscience et de mout bone. Mout volentiers se confessoit et souvent ausi comme chacun jour et mout devotement, et avoit acoutumé d'avoir a confessor mout bones persones et anciennes et mestres de dyvinité et tres grant reverence leur portoit. Et quant ele se confessoit ele se confessoit en sa chapele, et fessoit mout rev[er]anment[94] assoir son confessor devant li, pour ce qu'ele veist qu'il fust bien ententif a oïr sa confession et qu'il n'entendist a autre chosce et qu'il ne sonmillat. Ces chosces ele m'[a] dites[95] de sa bouche. Et autrement ele ne fut pas en pes de conscience s'ele ne fut certainne qu'il eut bien entendus ses pichiez, et mout tres humblement ele se tenoit devant son confessor quant ele se confessoit et ausi en tous autres leus,[96] et mout estoit obediens a lui pour nient[97] fut une[98] //(f. 131v) fame[99] de religion. Et avoit acutumé quant ele se confessoit que tousjour s'avoit[100] une dame et une damoisele un peu loing de li et de[101] disposition qu'eles pooient voir le confessor et li[102] quant ele se confessoit.[103]

[16] Souvent prenoit de mout grans deseplinnes, lesqueles madame Helins, de qui nous [avons] desus parlés qui longuement avoit esté avec li dont ele se fioit mout, li denoit[104] mout secrement. Ycele madame Helins quant ele la veoit deshestaie dissoit devant pluiseurs, "Dame,[105] vos deceplines

She would rise to say her matins well before daybreak and would not go back to bed at all and was continually in prayer right up to midday. And often she had those who served her eat before she did, in order to remain longer at her prayers. She did not speak at all when she would say her hours, nor before prime, nor after she had said compline, if she was not ill. She was wonderfully in prayer during Lent, more than at other times, and was often in a great abundance of tears, so that when she would come out of her oratory, she would have eyes so swollen and red that it was apparent that she had wonderfully shed tears. She was accustomed to be at prayer in her oratory right up to midday, and then she would go out from her oratory and into her chamber and then up to nones would be occupied with the study of holy writings, such as the Bible and the holy Gospels and other lives of the saints, because she understood Latin very well and understood it so well that when her chaplains had written her letters for her that she would have written in Latin, and they would bring them to her, she would amend them when there were any wrong words. And I, Sister Agnes of Harcourt, saw this many times and other people too. Wonderfully would she hear the word of our Lord, and often would have it said before her.

She was of very tender conscience and very good. Very willingly she would confess and often, even every day, and very devoutly. And she was accustomed to have for her confessors very good and aged people and masters of divinity, and she showed them very great reverence. And when she would confess herself, she would confess herself in her chapel and would reverently have her confessor sit before her so that she saw that he was really attentive to her confession and that he did not listen to other things and that he did not sleep. These things she told me with her own mouth. And otherwise her conscience had no peace if she was not certain that he had heard her sins well. And very humbly she would hold herself before her confessor when she confessed, and also in all other places, and would be very obedient to him as though she were a woman of religion. And she had this custom when she would confess that she would always have a lady and a damsel a little way from her and arranged so that they could see the confessor and her while she would confess.

Often she would take very great disciplines, which Madame Helen—of whom we have spoken above, who was with her for a long time [and] in whom she trusted greatly—would give her most secretly. This same Madame Helen, when she would see her undressed, would say before sev-

n'estoit pas comme autres, eles estoit juques au sanc." Ele prendoit ses deceplines non pas san plus de simples verches, mes de fracon dont sa raube estoit souvent tainte de sanc.

[17]   Ceste benoite dame visetoit humblement et charitablement en sa propre persone les malades, et les confortoit de ses saintes paroles, et leur amounetoit du salu[106] de leur ames, et les servoit de ses propres mains, et leu envoiet largement de ses biens, et mout longuement se seoit devant eux et tastoit leur pous. Mout avoit grand pitiet de ceux qui estoient en afflicion et avoit tres grant chalousie des salus[107] des ames.

[18]   Pour tout le monde ele ne dist[108] une fause parole a esciant. Nul serement je n'oï onques yssir de sa bouche; quant ele avoit dite une parole c'estoit sans rapeler, pour rens ele ne feist encontre. Mout s'estudioit d'acomplir //(f. 132r) les paroles de l'Evangile, especiaument yces[109] oeuvres de misericorde dont Nostre Seigneur dist en l'Evangile[110] qu'il se loera au general jugement.

[19]   Par grans tans aprés ce qu'ele avoit oït son office avant qu'ele dinast ele fesoit venir grand multitude de povres, si que sa chambre en estoit toute avironnee, et les servoit de ses pouvres[111] mains de pain, de vin, de potanche et de pitance, et mout se travailloit a ces chosces fere. Les grandes multitudes des aumosnes privees qu'ele fesoit et as regligeus[112] et aus seculeurs tant en i a c'on ne les[113] porroit raconter. Une damoisele bien gentius fame qui estoit apelé la damoisele de Meru estoit en une maladerie pres de li, laquele estoit mervilleusement deffaite. Madame en avoit tres grant pitiés[114] et estoit tres deligent de fere ce que besoing li estoit, et li envoiet les viandes de sa table et eslisoit de ses mains celes qu'ele pensoit qui milleurs li estoient et plus delicieuses, si diligement que pour nient fust ele sa file, et semblabes chosces fit ele pluseurs foi.

[20]   Ele fila de ses propres mains un cueuvrechief,[115] lequele le saint rois Loïs son freres li demanda et li pria mout gracieusement qu'ele li donnast et il le meteroit de nuit sour son chief. Ele ni li vaut donner, si comme je seur Agnez de Harecourt qui estoie presente l'oï de sa bouche de mes orilles. Ele respondi au roi et li dit,[116] "Je propose qu'il soit denez a Nostre Seigneur, car c'est le premier que je filasse onques." Et il li pria et[117] dit, "Seur, or vos pri je que vos en filez un autre que je aie." Et ele respondi, //(f. 132v) "Je le vuel bien, se j'en file plus." Et ce cueuvrechief ele envoya secreement[118] a une povre

eral other people, "Lady, your disciplines were not like the others, they were to the point of blood!" She would take her disciplines not only with simple rods but with a *fracon*,[5] from which her robe was often stained with blood.

This blessed lady humbly and charitably would visit the sick in her own person and would comfort them with her holy words and advise them on the salvation of their souls and serve them with her own hands and send to them generously of her goods and sit before them for a long time and feel their pulse. She had great pity for those who were afflicted and had great zeal for the salvation of souls.

For all the world she would not knowingly say a false word. I never heard any oath escape her mouth. When she had said a word, it was without recall, for nothing would she act against it. She strove greatly to accomplish the words of the Gospel, especially those works of mercy that our Lord says in the Gospel he will praise at the Last Judgment.[6]

For a great space of time after she had heard her office before she dined she would have a great multitude of poor people come, so that her chamber would be surrounded by them, and would serve them with her poor hands bread, wine, soup, [and] sustenance, and she worked hard to do these things. Of the great multitudes of private alms that she gave both to religious and to secular people there were so many that they could not be recounted. A damsel, a very noble woman, who was called the damsel of Meru, was in an infirmary near her and was truly reduced to a miserable state. Madame had great pity for her and was very concerned to do what was necessary for her and sent her food from her table and chose with her own hands those [foods] that she thought would be best for her and the most delicious, so diligently that she could have been her daughter, and similar things she did many times.

She sewed with her own hands a cap that the holy king Louis, her brother, asked her for, and he beseeched her most graciously that she would give it to him, and he would wear it on his head at night. She did not want to give it to him, as I, Sister Agnes of Harcourt, who was present, heard from her mouth with my own ears. She responded to the king and said, "I propose that it should be given to our Lord, because it is the first that I have ever sewn." And he beseeched her and said, "Sister, then I beseech you that you sew another one that I might have." And she responded, "I

fame qui gissoit en grant langueur, laquele ele visitoit tres soigneusement
jascun jour de[119] grans benefices de sa table et d'especiaus viandes. Dame Je-
205   henne et dame Perronele de Montfort entendirent ceste chosce de ce
cuevrechief et alerent a la pouvre fame secreement et l'achaterent[120] et li en
denerent tant comme elle vaut prendre, et est a nonnains de Saint Antoynes
et le gardent comme reliques.

[21]   Monsieur le roi Loïs son pere, qui mourut en Montpencier,[121]
210   li laissa mout grans deniers quant il morut, et tout ele dena pour Diu, et especiaument ele envoya dix chevaliers outre mer. Ele assena tant de persones en religion que nous n'en savons nul nombre. Mout fesoit de biens
et d'aumosnes a veves fames et a orfenins. Et mervilleusement avoit grant
compassion de gens qui estoient a mesaise et en affliction. Ele avoit ceste
215   coutume le jeudy absolut qu'ele prenoit xiii pouvres et leur lavoit leurs piés,
et les servoit de ses propres mains de deus pere de mes, et leur denoit soulers
et offroit a chascun xxx parisis en remembrance du pris que Nostre Seigneur
fu vendus.
[22]   Mout estoit en grant estude de fere chosce qui pleust a Nostre
220   Seigneur et ot mout grant volenté de fere un hospital, et ne savoit ce qu'ele[122]
en deust fere, ou une maison de nostre ordene ou un hospital. Elle envoya au
chancelier de Paris et li fit demander secreement lequel il //(f. 133r) quidoit
qui plairoit plus a Deu, ou qu'ele fondast un hospital ou une maison de
s[e]reurs meneurs. Li chancelers Hemery, qui estoit mout preudome et
225   mestres de divinités qui adonc estoit son confessor, li manda que ce n'estoit
mie comparissons[123] de l'hospital au regart de fere meson[124] de religion, et
especiaument de cel ordre, car la devine loenge Nostre Seigneur i est fete et
celebré, et virginitez i est gardee et moutepllé et avec ce les euvres de misericorde i sont fetes, car les s[e]reurs servent a[125] l'une l'autre. Et dit encore au
230   messaige, "Dites li qu'ele ne demande plus consel de cet chosce,[126] mes face
la meson de religion." Et tantost aprés elle fonda nostre abbeÿe, laquele
qui[127] cousta bien trente mille livres de parisis.

[23]   Ele fu tres deligent de la riule qu'ele fust bone et seure, et la fist
esprouver par freres meneurs qui estoit persones bones et esprouvees et
235   mestres de divinité, si comme frere Bone aventure,[128] frere Guillaume de
Miletonne, et frere Eude de Rony, et frere Geffroy de Vierson, frere Guillaume de Hartembour, et fist metre en la riule ce qui estoit es[129] previ-

would be pleased to do that if I sew more." And she sent this cap secretly to a poor woman who lay in great distress, whom she visited with great care each day with great benefits from her table and special dishes. Lady Jeanne and Lady Perronelle of Montfort heard of this affair of the cap and went to the poor woman secretly and bought it and gave her as much as she would take for it, and it belongs to the nuns of Saint Antoine, and they guard it as a relic.

Monsieur the king Louis, her father, who died at Montpencier, left her a great amount of money when he died, and she gave it all for God, and especially she sent ten knights overseas. She placed so many people in religion that we do not know the number of them. She gave many goods and alms to widowed women and orphans. And she had wonderfully great compassion for people who were in pain and affliction. She had this custom that on Maundy Thursday she would take thirteen poor people and wash their feet and serve them with her own hands with two pairs of dishes and would give them shoes and would offer to each thirty Parisian sous in remembrance of the price for which our Lord was sold.

She was very anxious to do something that would be pleasing to our Lord and had a great desire to found a hospital, but did not know what she ought to make of this, whether a house of our order or a hospital. She sent to the chancellor of Paris and had him asked secretly which he thought would be more pleasing to God, whether she should found a hospital or a house of Sisters Minor. The chancellor Aymeric, who was a wise man and master of divinity, who was then her confessor, wrote to her that there was no comparison with a hospital when it came to founding a house of religion, and especially of this order, because the divine praise of our Lord is carried out and celebrated there, and virginity is guarded and multiplied there, and also works of charity are done there, since the sisters serve one another. And he further said to the messenger, "Tell her that she should not demand further counsel on this matter, but build the house of religion." And soon after she founded our abbey, which indeed cost her[7] thirty thousand Parisian livres.

She was very diligent as to the rule, that it should be good and sure, and had it approved by Brothers Minor, who were good people and mature and masters of divinity, such as Brother Bonaventure, Brother William of Meliton, Brother Eudes of Rosny, Brother Geoffrey of Vierson, and Brother William of Harcombourg, and she had put into the rule what

leges;[130] et ce qui estoit[131] doutable et p[e]rilleux en la riule ele fist oster. Et estoit en si grant estiude de cette chosce qu'ele en villoit grant partie des nuis et de jour. Elle i travella tant et estudia qu'a painnes[132] le poiroit on raconter. Pluseurs persones estoient en sa chambre de queus aucuns lisoient les previleges et les autres notoient, et estoit tousjours illec un[133] frere meneurs //(f. 133v) mestres de divinité pour examiner les chosces devant li[134] en sa presence. Et tant estoit en grant soin que rien ne passast qui fust p[e]rilleux as[135] ames si que c'estoit mervele. Et de ceste chosce elle estoit en si grant soin et en si grant estoide que a painnes pooit ele repauser.

[24] Et mervilleusement eut[136] avoit grant deisier que ceste chosce fust confermee de l'apoitoile.[137] Et sour toutes chosces elle voloit que les s[e]rurs de s'abeÿe fuissent apelees s[e]rurs meneurs. Et en nulle maniere la riule ne li pooit souffire[138] se ce nom n'i fust mis. Son benoit cuer eslut a metre en s'abeÿe ce benoit non, ouquels[139] Nostre Seigneur Jesu Crit eslut Nostre Dame a estre sa mere. C'est le non de L'Humilité Nostre Dame qu'ele mit non a s'abbeÿe, et de ce non elle vaut qu'ele fust nommee. Et[140] je seur Agnes de Harecourt li demandai, "Dame, dites moy pour Diu, si vous plet, pourcoi[141] vous avez mis ce non en vostre[142] abbeÿe." Elle me respondi, "Pour ce que je n'oï onques parler de nulle persone qui le preist, dont je me mervel qu'i[143] me semble qu'ils ont lessiés le plus haut non et le meilleur qu'il peuissent prendre, et si est le non par quel[144] Nostre Seigneur eslut Nostre Dame a estre sa mere. Et pour ce l'é ge pris a metre a ma meson."

[25] Elle fu malade de grans maladies avant que la riule fust confermee, qu'ele estoit ausi comme en langueur de cuer dusques adonc que cest chosce fu acomplie. //(f. 134r) Par[145] grand sens et par grant humilitez ele ne voloit riens recreire a l'apotoile, ne escrire pour chosce qui apartenist a sa riule ne a s'abbaÿe, et non feissoit elle neys[146] de nulle grant besoigne qu'ele eust affere, mes toutes ces chosces elle feissoit requere par monseigneur le roi Loïs son frere qu'ele[147] feissoit chievetain de toutes ses besoinges, et il le feissoit mout courtoissement et envoyet ses letres et ses[148] prop[r]es messagez. Et cele coutume elle avoit, que quant son saint frere le roi Loïs venoit[149] en liu ou elle estoit, elle l'alloit saluer et s'agenouloit devant li de la grant reverence qu'ele avoit a li, et il la relevoit par les mains et li blasmoit, et[150] li desplaissoit mout ce paroit, mes elle n'en voloit riens lessier.

was in the privileges, and what was doubtful or perilous in the rule she eliminated, and she had such great concern for this matter that she stayed up a large part of the nights and days. She worked and devoted herself so much to this that it can hardly be recounted. Many people were in her chamber, of which some would read the privileges and the others would note them, and there was always present a Brother Minor, master of divinity, to examine the matters before her in her presence. And she was so concerned that nothing should pass that would be perilous to souls that it was a wonder. And she took such great care with this matter and was so involved that she could hardly rest.

And she had a wonderfully great desire that this matter should be confirmed by the pope. And above all things she desired that the sisters of her abbey would be called Sisters Minor. And in no way could the rule be acceptable to her if this name was not given. Her blessed heart chose to give to her abbey this blessed name by which our Lord Jesus Christ chose our Lady to be his mother.[8] It is the name of The Humility of Our Lady that she gave as name to her abbey, and with this name she desired that it should be named. And I, Sister Agnes of Harcourt, asked her, "Lady, tell me please, for God's sake, why you have given this name to your abbey?" She responded to me, "Because I have never heard tell of any person who took it, which surprises me, for it seems to me that they have left out the highest name and the best that they could take, since it is the name by which our Lord chose our Lady to be his mother. And for this I have taken it to give to my house."

She was gravely ill before the rule was confirmed, so that it was as though she were languishing in her heart until this affair was accomplished. Out of great sense and great humility she did not want to request anything of the pope or write concerning matters that pertained to her rule or to her abbey, and she would not do anything concerning any great affair that she had to do, but all these things she would cause to be requested by Monseigneur the king Louis, her brother, whom she made chief of all her affairs, and he would do it most courteously and would send his letters and his own messages. And she had this custom that when her holy brother, the king Louis, would come to the place where she was, she would go to greet him and kneel down before him out of the great reverence that she had for him, and he would raise her with his hands and rebuke

[26] Mervilleusement parloit petit et mout tenoit de silence, et quant elle parloit c'estoit mout priement[151] et mout apenseement. Et aucunes fois frere Eude de Roni son confessor li dissoit, "Dame, y fust[152] bien que vous parlissiez[153] et que vous vous esbatissiez, y[154] ne depleust pas a Nostre Seigneur se vous prissiez un peu de recreation," et li demandoit pourcoi elle tenoit tant silence. Elle li dissoit que c'estoit[155] pour ce qu'ele avoit aucune fois trop parlés et dites[156] paroles oiseuses, si estoit bon qu'ele en feist la penitence. Mout avoit de parlemens a son confessor des biens de vie parneble[157] et des devinnes escritures. Mout avoit grant reverence a Nostre Seigneur et mout le tremoit,[158] si comme elle me conta une fois secreement, a mai et a li, que quant elle //(f. 134v) estoit revenue de sa chapele d'oroissons et ele estoit seur son lit apoié,[159] il li remembra des jugemens Nostre Seigneur, elle me dit qu'ele trambloit si fort que la robe et le fueire trambloit desous li forment.

[27] Et aucunes fois vi je que d'auqu[n]es chosces qui li desplaissoient, elle blasmoit forment aucunes persones devant[160] mai, seur Agnes de Harecourt, et ce pourcoi elle les blasmoit si estoit pour aucunes bones oeuvres qu'eles[161] n'avoient pas fetes qu'ele leur avoit encharchiez. Et pour ce qu'il[162] li sambloit[163] qu'ele avoit parlé trop aprement, elle leur dissoit sa coulpe devant mai mervilleusement humblement, et mout s'acussoit et recordoit les paroles qu'ele avoit dites en agrigant sur li. Mout me feissoit grant bien a l'oïr,[164] et puis m'en a fait bien la remembrance maintes fois. Je cro qu'i n'est nul picheur[165] encore[166] qui euist fet neys[167] mout de pichiés mourteux, se[168] il s'umilioit tant devant Diu et euist aussi[169] grant repentance comme elle avoit quant elle avoit dit aucune chosce ou elle se doutoit que il n'i eust pichiez neys ou il n'en[170] avoit point, si crioit a Diu mercy qu'il n'eust largement misericorde, tant doutoit a courroucier Nostre Seigneur et se gardoit de toutes achoisons en soy et en autruy.

[28] Et ot[171] sa fin de grant[172] maladies deux ans avant qu'ele trespassat, lesqueles elle receut de son doux espoux tres doucement, et en grant patience les porta. //(f. 135r) Et tres devotement sa vie fina, en parfaite virginité et en[173] tres[174] grant humilité et charité.

her, and it appeared that this displeased him greatly, but she did not want to cease.

She spoke wonderfully little and greatly kept her silence, and when she spoke it was very kindly and thoughtfully. And sometimes Brother Eudes of Rosny, her confessor, would say to her, "Lady, it would be well if you spoke and amused yourself, it would not displease our Lord if you were to take a little recreation," and he would ask her why she kept such silence. She would tell him that it was because she had sometimes spoken too much and said idle words, so it was good that she should do penance for them. She had many conversations with her confessor concerning the good things of eternal life and divine Scripture. She had a great reverence for our Lord and feared him greatly; she recounted to me once secretly, to me and to him, that when she had returned from her prayer chapel, and she was leaning on her bed, she remembered the judgment of our Lord; she told me that she trembled so hard that the bedclothes and the bedstraw trembled mightily beneath her.

And sometimes I saw that for some things that displeased her she would strongly reprimand some people before me, Sister Agnes of Harcourt. And the reason why she would reprimand them thus was for certain good works that they had not done with which she had charged them. And since it seemed to her that she had spoken too sharply, she would admit to them her fault before me wonderfully humbly, and she would accuse herself very much and recall the words that she had said, making them [appear] worse. It did me much good to hear her, and since then the memory has done me good many times. I believe that there is no sinner who has committed no matter how many mortal sins—if he humbled himself as much before God and would have as great repentance as she had when she had said anything in which she would wonder whether there was not some sin (when really there was none)—if he would cry for mercy to God, that he would not generously receive mercy, so much did she fear to anger our Lord and guard herself against all occasions for offense in herself and in others.

And she had her final great maladies two years before she died, which she received from her sweet groom very sweetly and bore in great patience. And very devoutly her life ended, in perfect virginity and in very great humility and charity.

De ses miracles[175]

305   [1]   Quant nostre tres reverent et sainte dame et mere vivoit, un des ser-
gens monsiegneur le roi Loïs avoit un enfant qui cheoit de la grant maladie.
Yceys hons pria en grans larmes a genous et a mains jointes devotement a la
sainte dame qu'ele priast Dieu pour son enfant qui estoit si cruellement
malades. Et ele s'enclina en signe qu'ele en prieret Nostre Seigneur. Li peres
310 s'en ala a son hostel et trouva que son enfant estoit gueris et n'avoit plus cele
maladie. Il retourna a madame et s'agellongua devant li et dit, "Ma douce
dame, vous souvint il de ce que je vous requis? Pour Dieu, dites moy se vous
en priates Nostre Seigneur." Elle li respondi, "Oïl." Lors il li dit, "Ma douce
dame, je ren graces a Dieu et a vous que mon enfant est gueri et je tieng fer-
315 mement que c'est par vos prieres." Et elle li dit, "Non, ne tenez pas que ce
soit par moy; je ne suis pas telle que Diex face tiex[176] choses par[177] moy." Et
il li diset toujours qu'il tenet que c'estet par ses merites et par ses prieres.
Quant ele vit que ele ne le poet a ce metre qu'il ne tenit que c'estoit par li, si
li deffendi et li fit creancer qu'il n'en diset riens tant comme ele fut en vie.
320 Madame la grant reyne Marguerite nous conta cette chose et dit que li hons
qui estoit peres a l'enfant li conta cete chose en verité.

    [2]   Encore quant madame vivoit seur Aalis de Mucedent[178] fu mout
malade d'une fievre tierçaine. Ele ot devotion a madame, et li estoit avis
que se madame priat[179] pour li que ele fut guerie.[180] //(f. 135v) Icelle suer
325 Aalis requit a seur Agnes d'Anery, qui adonc estoit abbesse, que ele y alat.
Elle n'y osa aler por sa[181] reverence. Seur Alis en pria seur Agnes de Harecourt; elle y ala et li montra la fiance que la malade y avoit. La sainte dame
regarda seur Agnes de Harecourt et sousrit mout amiablement, et tost aprés
la malade fu toute guerie de sa fievre. Je suer Agnes de Harecour qui portay
330 la parole suy tesmong[182] de cete chose, et aussi seur Agnes d'Anery vit toutes
ces choses.

    [3]   Seur Sare de Houpelines ot une maladie mout perilleuse que l'en
apele l'orguelleux. Son cors estoit tout entrepris de boces et de taches, et
cuidoit l'en que ele deut morir. Madame nostre sainte mere vint devers nous
335 et la regarda piteusement et toucha la maladie de ses benaites mains, et tan-

Of Her Miracles

When our very reverend and holy lady and mother was alive, one of the sergeants of Monseigneur the king Louis had a child who had fallen ill with a great malady. This man prayed on his knees with great tears and with joined hands devotedly to the holy lady, that she should pray to God for his child who was so cruelly ill, and she nodded as a sign that she would pray to our Lord for him. The father went to his lodging and found that his child was cured and no longer had the malady. He returned to Madame and kneeled before her and said, "My gentle lady, do you remember what I requested of you? For God's sake, tell me if you prayed for him to our Lord." She responded to him, "Yes." Then he said to her, "My gentle lady, I give thanks to God and to you that my child is cured, and I believe firmly that it is through your prayers." And she said to him, "No, do not believe that it is through me, I am not such that God would do these things through me." And he still told her that he believed that it was through her merits and through her prayers. When she saw that she could not bring about that he would not believe that it was through her, she forbade him to [say anything] and had him promise that he would not say anything as long as she lived. Madame the great queen Marguerite recounted this affair to us and said that the man who was the father of the child recounted the affair to her in truth.

Also, while Madame was alive, Sister Alice of Mucedent was very ill with a tertian fever.[9] She had devotion to Madame and believed that if Madame prayed for her that she would be cured. This same Sister Alice requested of Sister Agnes of Anery, who was abbess at the time, that she should go to her. She did not dare to go to her because of her reverence. Sister Alice asked Sister Agnes of Harcourt; she went to her and related the faith that the sick woman had in her. The holy lady looked at sister Agnes of Harcourt and smiled most amiably, and soon afterward the sick woman was entirely cured of her fever. I, Sister Agnes of Harcourt, who carried the message, am witness to this matter, and Sister Agnes of Anery also saw all these things.

Sister Sara of Houpelines had a very dangerous illness that is called the *orguelleux*.[10] Her body was all covered with spots and blotches, and it was thought that she would die. Madame our holy mother came among us and looked pityingly at her and touched the malady with her blessed hands, and

tost aprés la seur fu toute guerie. De cete chose plusieurs sereurs sont tesmong[183] qui la virent malade et guerie.

[4] Frere Denyses d'Estampes de l'ordre des freres meneurs, qui demeuroit en cete abeÿe pour administrer les sacremens as sereurs, ot fievre
340   quartaine par lonc tans. Il fu presens avec les autres freres meneurs quant on enolia madame nostre sainte mere, et yce jour estoit le jour de sa fievre. Il fu gueris de sa fievre par les merites de la sainte dame et onques puis n'ot fievre quartaine, et vesqui puys lonc tans. Cete[184] chose il raconta a plusieurs sereurs et afferma estre vraie, et li convens le vit malade et gueri.

345   [5] Seur Erembour de Cerceles dit en verité que en icele nuit que nostre benaite dame trespassa, elle oÿ devant matines une voix qui li dit, "In pace factus est locus ejus." Et tantost ycele seur Erembour ala a l'abbeesse et li dit que ele avoit ainsit oÿ, l'en trouva que la saint dame estoit trespassé, u[185] estoit u tret de la mort, et que c'estoit chose veritable de son trespas en ycele
350   heure. //(f. 136r) Et semblablement en icelle heure seur Jehane de Louveçainnes oÿt tele meymes voix.

[6] Suer Climence[186] d'Argas dit en verité[187] que la nuyt que nostre sainte et reverent dame et mere trespassa, un po devant matines ele ouvri la fenestre qui estoit delez[188] son lit en entention por savoir[189] se elle oÿroit
355   nului[190] en la court,[191] quar ele savoit bien que madame estoit pres de sa fin, et regardoit l'er qui estoit tres bel et tres seri. Ele oÿ une voix mout douce et mout melodieuse sus la meson u[192] ele gisoit, et l'oÿ si longuement que il[193] li semble en verité que ele n'oÿ onques si longue alaine en cete mortel vie. Ycele seur Climence mit son chief hors des fers de la fenestre pour miex
360   savoir[194] que[195] c'estoit et tantost[196] aprés ce l'en sonna matines et nous aporta l'en la nouvelle que madame nostre sainte mere estoit trespassee.

[7] Aussi seur Aveline de Hennaut en cele heure oÿ chans mout doux et mout melodieux et se leva en son seant en son lit, mes ele ne sot que ce fu. Nous creons fermement que c'estoit la melodie des sains angeles qui con-
365   duisoient sa benoite ame en la gloire du ciel, car ele avoit loyaument honneré Dieu et servi en sa vie.

[8] Quant nostre sainte dame ot esté en terre par neuf jours, au neuvime jour on la leva de la sepulture pour metre en un autre sarcu plus convenable que celui u ele estoit. Elle ne senti nule mauvese oudeur, ains paroit
370   ausi come se ele dormit. Elle avoit les membres si biaus,[197] si plains et si

soon after the sister was entirely cured. Several sisters who saw her sick and cured are witnesses to this matter.

Brother Denis of Etampes of the Order of Brothers Minor, who was living in this abbey to administer the sacraments to the sisters, had the quartan fever[11] for a long time. He was present with the other Brothers Minor when Madame our holy mother received extreme unction, and this day was the day of his fever. He was cured of his fever by the merits of the holy lady and never afterward had the quartan fever and lived for a long time. He recounted this affair to several sisters and affirmed it to be true, and the convent saw him sick and cured.

Sister Erembour of Cerceles says in truth that on the same night that our blessed lady passed away, she heard before matins a voice that said to her, "In peace her place has been prepared."[12] And as soon as this same Sister Erembour went to the abbess and told her that she had heard this, it was found that the holy lady had passed away or was on the verge of death, and her death in this same hour was certain. And similarly in this same hour Sister Jeanne of Louveciennes heard the same voice.

Sister Clemence of Argas says in truth that the night that our holy and reverend lady and mother passed away, a little before matins she opened the window, which was next to her bed, wanting to know if she could hear anyone in the courtyard, because she well knew that Madame was near her end, and she was regarding the air, which was very lovely and serene. She heard a very sweet and melodious voice above the house where she was lying, and heard it so long that it seemed to her truly that she had never heard so long a breath in this mortal life. This same Sister Clemence put her head outside the bars of the window to find out what it was, and soon after this matins was sounded, and we were brought the news that Madame our holy mother had passed away.

Also Sister Aveline of Hainault at this hour heard very sweet and very melodious singing and got up, sitting on her bed, but she did not know what it was. We believe firmly that it was the melody of the holy angels who were conducting her blessed soul to the glory of heaven, because she had loyally honored and served God in her life.

When our holy lady had been in the ground for nine days, on the ninth day she was raised from her tomb to put her in another coffin more suitable than the one in which she was. She did not give off any bad odor, and she looked just as though she were sleeping. She had limbs as pretty and as

traitables et si maniables comme d'un tendre enfant, et la face li resplendis-
soit mervelleusement, si que toutes ces choses estoit mervelleuses a regarder.
Et par ce que on la demena tant li eus[198] li ouvrirent, liquel estoient si bel
sans blesmir et sans muer que il ne sembloit pas que il fussent estaint de
375   mort. Nous la //(f. 136v) devestimes de la robe que ele avoit eu neuf jours en
terre qui estoit si belle et si nette que il ne sembloit pas que ele eust onques
esté vestue. Pour ce que nous voliens avoir cele robe comme reliques, nous la
revestimes de nouvelle robe et la traitiens[199] tout ainsi comme nous voliens.
Ce vit li convent et madame la contesse de Flandres Marguerite, et ma-
380   dame Marie sa fille qui est nonnain, et la dame d'Audenarde et plusieurs
autres persones, et dame Huloÿs la veve bourgoise de Paris[200] et monseigneur Guillaume de Quitry[201] chanoine de Vernon qui fu son chapelain,
et 2[202] maçons[203] qui estoient illec pour mettre le sarcu, et toutes ces persones
estoit dedans l'enclos. Par dehors a la fenestre furent tant de persones qui la
385   virent, que nous n'en sarions dire le nombre et de religion et du siecle, entre
lesquex furent frere Eude de Rooni mestre de divinité qui fu son confessor,
frere Pierre de Meurevile,[204] frere Thomas du Plexi, frere Giles de Sally et
plusieurs autres freres meneurs. Et y estoit madame la fille au conte de Flandres[205] qui fu duchesse de Braban et plusieurs autres dames et chevaliers et
390   bourgois et menu pueple. Nous ouvrimes la fenestre du moustier et levasmes
le coffre et leur montrasmes la sainte dame comme un enfant en son berceul.
Ils s'efforçoient qui miex miex de baller leurs cuevrechiefs, leur aniaus,
leur fermans, leur chapiaux, leur çaintures, leur aumosnieres pour touchier
au saint cors par grant devotion, et ce qui y avoit touchié il[206] tenoient a
395   reliques.

        [9]   Icis freres[207] de cui nous avons dessus parlé raconta de sa bouche
que aprés huit jours que cete nostre sainte dame et mere fu trespassee, il cou-
vroit les autiex de nostre eglise en queresme et une mout grant table qui
estoit a l'autel monseigneur Saint Pere chey sur luy. Il estoit si[208] febles que
400   de sa force il n'ot //(f. 137r) pooir de soi lever et fu dessous le fes par lonc
espace de tans. En ce peril et en cele mesaise il requit l'ayde de nostre sainte
dame, et tantost il se leva legierement de dessous ce grant fes sans avoir nule
bleceure et fit son office viguereusement si comme devant. Cete chose il
raconta a plusieurs sereurs qui en furent[209] tesmong.[210]

405   [10]   Frere[211] Giles de Sally, qui fu par lonc tans avec frere Eude de Roni,
avoit un cuevrechief que cete sainte dame ot sus son chief en sa darreniere
maladie et y sua la sueur de la mort. Il estoit malade de fievre tiercienne. Il

plump and as flexible and as manageable as those of a tender child, and her face shone wonderfully, so that all these things were wonderful to behold. And because she was moved about so much, her eyes opened, which were so pretty, without turning pale or changing, that it did not seem that they were dimmed by death. We removed the robe that she had had on for nine days in the ground, which was so pretty and so clean that it did not seem that it had ever been worn. Since we wanted to have this robe as a relic, we dressed her again in a new robe, and we treated it entirely as we wished. The convent saw this, and Madame the countess of Flanders Marguerite, and Madame Marie, her daughter, who is a nun, and the Lady of Audenarde, and many other people, and Lady Helois, the bourgeois widow of Paris, and Monseigneur William of Quitry, canon of Vernon, who was her chaplain, and the two masons who were there to set the coffin, and all these people were in the enclosure. Outside at the window were so many people who saw her that we could not count them, both religious and secular, among whom were Brother Eudes of Rosny, master of divinity, who was her confessor, Brother Pierre of Meureville, Brother Thomas of Plexi, Brother Giles of Sally and many other Brothers Minor. And there was Madame the daughter of the count of Flanders, who was the duchess of Brabant, and many other ladies and knights and city people and common people. We opened the window of the monastery and lifted the chest and showed them the holy lady like an infant in its cradle. They strove as best they could to dangle their caps, their rings, their broaches, their hats, their belts, their purses to touch the holy body through great devotion, and what had touched it they kept as relics.

This brother, of whom we have spoken above, told with his own mouth that eight days after our holy lady and mother had died, he was covering the altars of our church for Lent, and a very large table, which was at the altar of Monseigneur Saint Peter, fell on him. He was so feeble that with his own power he could not lift it off him and was under this weight for a long time. In this peril and in this tribulation he asked the aid of our holy lady, and at once he got up easily from under this great weight with no injury and performed his office vigorously as before. This affair he recounted to several sisters, who were witnesses to it.

Brother Giles of Sally, who was for a long time with Brother Eudes of Rosny, had a cap that this holy lady had on her head during her final illness and in it had sweated the sweat of death. He was ill from the tertian

mit par devotion de la sainte ce cuevrechief sus son chief et tantost il com-
mença a suer et fu gueris. Seur Agnes d'Anery, seur Marie de Cambrai, seur
Marie de Tremblay oÿrent cete chose de la bouche a ce frere Giles et en sunt
tesmong.[212]

[11] Seur Ade de Rains dit en verité que une truye li empira[213] un
des dois de sa main en tele maniere que ele n'ot point de ongle en ce doit
par 20 ans et plus. Quant madame nostre reverent et sainte mere fu enterree,
ycete seur Ade prit de la terre entour le cors et la lia sur ce doit et li tint par
neuf[214] jours. Au neuvime jour ele le delia; il fu si tres purement gueris que
y n'i[215] paret qu'il y eust onques eu mal et ot bel ongle et entier qui point
n'en avoit devant, et fu[216] sain toute sa vie. Li convens vit le doit malade
et sain.

[12] Seur Ermesent de Paris demoura une fois toute seule u moustier
sans congié quant li convens mengoit au souper en la nouvelleté que
madame nostre benaite mere fu trespassee. Une tres grant doleur la prit en
son chief et[217] y sentoit avec[218] trop grant ardeur. Et en cete doleur une grant
poour la prit de ce que ele estoit demouree sans congié, et pensa que ele iroit
en refiectoir avec les sereurs, et[219] li vint une //(f. 137v) grant volenté en son
cuer aussi comme se ce fut une creature qui parlat a son cuer, et li deyt, "Non
feras, mes va a ta sainte dame et li requier ayde." Ele y ala et se bouta desous
une fourme qui estoit sur le cors et jotit[220] son chief et sa joe a la terre qui
estoit dessus le cors et la pria mout diligemment a grand efforcement, a
grans larmes par longue piece et au darrenier[221] ele s'endormi[222] illec. Quant
ele se leva ele se trouva toute guerie. Je seur Agnes de Harecourt qui adonc
estoie en l'office d'abbeesse porte tesmong de cete chose. Car icele seur Er-
mensent vint tantost a moy aussi comme tout effree, et me dit que a po
qu'ele n'avoit perdu son sens par[223] la doleur que ele avoit eu en son chief et
de la poeur que ele avoit eu, se Diex et madame ne l'eussent guerie. Seur
Mahaut d'Escoce,[224] seur Marie de Cambray et plusieurs autres sereurs por-
tent tesmong de cete chose.

[13] Une autre de nos sereurs perdi son sens si outreement et fu si
frenetique que quant ele poet eschaper d'entre celes qui la gardoient, ele
montoit sur les bans et sur les huches et rampoit ez[225] parois pour prendre les
yregnees. Et quanques[226] ele[227] en poet prendre ele les manget, et se boutoit
dessous les tables et queroit yregnés et barbelotes ecloses, et par tout u ele les

fever. He put this cap on his head out of devotion to the saint, and soon he began to sweat and was cured. Sister Agnes of Anery, Sister Marie of Cambrai, and Sister Marie of Tremblay heard this affair from the mouth of this Brother Giles and are witnesses to it.

Sister Ade of Reims says in truth that a sow harmed one of the fingers of her hand in such a manner that she had no nail on this finger for twenty years or more. When Madame our reverend and holy mother was buried, this same Sister Ade took some of the earth from around the body and bound it on her finger and kept it there for nine days. On the ninth day she removed it; it was so perfectly cured that it did not appear that there had ever been an injury, and she had a pretty and entire nail that she had certainly not had before, and it was healthy her whole life. The convent saw the finger injured and healthy.

Sister Ermesent of Paris once remained all alone in the church without permission while the convent was eating supper, just after our blessed mother had passed away. A great pain took her in her head, and she felt it with great force. And in this pain a great fear took her since she had remained behind without permission, and she thought that she would go to the refectory with the sisters. And there came to her a great desire in her heart as though it was someone that spoke to her heart and said, " Do not do it, but rather go to your holy lady and ask her for help." She went there and squeezed herself under a bench that was over the body and touched her head and her cheek to the ground that was over the body and prayed to her most diligently with great force [and] with great tears for a long time, and finally she fell asleep there. When she arose, she found herself entirely cured. I, Sister Agnes of Harcourt, who then held the office of abbess, bear witness to this matter, since this same Sister Ermesent came right away to me as though quite afraid and told me that she would almost have lost her senses because of the pain that she had had in her head and the fear that she had had, if God and Madame had not cured her. Sister Mahaut of Scotland, Sister Marie of Cambrai, and several other sisters bear witness to this matter.

Another one of our sisters lost her senses so completely and was so frenzied that when she could escape from those who were guarding her, she would get up on the benches and on the chests and climb on the walls to catch spiders, and when she could catch them, she ate them. And she would squeeze herself under the tables and look for freshly hatched spiders

poet trouver[228] ele les[229] mengoit, et mout d'autres ordures que nous ne
volons pas nommer ele[230] menget[231] par[232] la grant fourcenerie u ele estoit. Et
445 en cete[233] maladie madame nostre benoiste mere, qui adonc vivet, la visita
mout humblement et en avoit mout grant compassion. Et cette maladie
dura a cele seur trois mois et demy puis que nostre sainte dame fu trespassee.
En l'amena une nuit a la tumbe[234] de la sainte et y vella toute la nuyt, et les
sereurs avec li qui furent en oraisons et //(f. 138r) priaient madame pour li
450 que ele la vosit sauver[235] de cele maladie. Tout ainsi comme la nuyt s'en alet,
son sens li revenoit, et a la journee ele ot son sens si apertement comme ele
avoit[236] onques eu, et onques puys n'en chey en cele maladie. Li convens vit
cette chose et en est temong.

[14]   Seur Julienne dit en verité que ele estoit en[237] chaleur de fievre et en
455 cele chaleur ele ot tres grand desirier de boivre par devotion au hennab[238] u
nostre sainte dame buvet en sa vie. Si tost comme ele y ot[239] beu, ele fu
alegiee de la chaleur de la fievre et fu assés tost toute guerie et plus de dix ans
aprés ele ne senti fievre.

[15]   Icele meymes seur Julienne avoit un livre lequel ele amoit mout
460 pour la devotion de ce qu'il avoit esté[240] nostre sainte dame. Ycis livres fu
perdus par male garde, de quoi elle fu mout mesaisiee. Ele alla a sa tumbe et
li requit mout a certes en pleurant que ele li rendit, quar ele l'amoit miex
pour ce qu'il avoit esté siens. Nostre douce sainte mere li aparut en dormant
et li dit que li livres estoit perdus et que ele en requeyt monsegneur le roi
465 Saint Loÿs son frere. Quant la seur s'esvella, elle fit s'oraison au saint et
proumit[241] au saint une livre de cire par le congié de l'abbeesse et tantost
comme on alla querre le livre en le trouva et par plusieurs jours devant ce on
ne le poet trouver et si l'avoit l'en mout quys.

[16]   Seur Ermengare de Chartres avoit une mout forte fievre tierçaine,
470 si ot[242] volenté et devotion de fere[243] une chandele de son lonc a madame
et la requit. Elle fu guerie mout netement de sa fievre, si que onques
puys n'en ot point. Elle ala a la tumbe et fit s'offrande le plus tost que ele
pot. //(f. 138v)

[17]   Madame la grant reine Marguerite, mere au[244] roi de France, fit
475 apporter monsegneur Phelippe le fil au roy qui fievre avoit en esperance
qu'i[245] fut gueris. Ele le fit couchier aupres la tumbe nostre sainte dame sa

and ants, and anywhere that she could find them she would eat them. And she ate many other filthy things that we do not wish to name, because of the great derangement in which she was. And in this malady Madame our blessed mother, who was then living, visited her most humbly and had great compassion for her. And this malady lasted for this sister three and a half months after our holy lady had passed away. She was brought one night to the tomb of the saint and there maintained a vigil the whole night, and the sisters with her, who were in prayer, prayed to Madame for her that she would save her from this malady. Just as the night disappeared, her senses came back to her, and at daytime she possessed her senses as sharply as she ever had and never afterward fell into this malady again. The convent saw this affair and is witness to it.

Sister Julienne says in truth that she was in the heat of a fever, and in this heat she had a great desire out of devotion to drink from the cup from which our holy lady drank during her life. As soon as she drank from it, she was relieved of the heat of the fever and was soon entirely cured, and more than ten years later she had experienced no fever.

This same Sister Julienne had a book that she loved very much out of devotion since it had belonged to our holy lady. This book was lost through carelessness, at which she was very disturbed. She went to her tomb and asked her, indeed crying, that she return it to her, because she loved it more since it had been hers. Our gentle holy mother appeared to her while she was sleeping and told her that the book was lost and that she should entreat Monseigneur the king Saint Louis, her brother, about it. When the sister woke up, she prayed to the saint and promised the saint a pound of wax, with the abbess's permission. And soon when the book was searched for it was found, and for several days before this it could not be found, although it was searched for diligently.

Sister Ermengarde of Chartres had a very high tertian fever, so that she had the desire and devotion to make a candle of her own height for Madame and entreated her. She was cured entirely of her fever so that she never afterward had one. She went to the tomb and made her offering as soon as she could.

Madame the dowager queen Marguerite, mother of the king of France, had brought Monseigneur Philip, the son of the king, who had a fever, in hopes that he would be cured. She had him laid near the tomb of our

reverent tante. Il fu gueris si comme il meymes apuys dit devant plusieurs sereurs que ele le gueri[246] et dit que s'en[247] souvien bien.[248]

[18] Seur Marguerite de Guyse avoit une buchette en l'un de ses yex; ele estoit a tele angoisse que ele ne poet ouvrir l'eul. Ele requit madame que ele li aydat et mit sus son eul des vestemens de la benoite sainte et tantost ele fu guerie.

[19] Seur Marie de Cambray avoit si perdue l'oÿe que ele n'oet aussi[249] comme nule goute[250] et ne savoit respondre a ce que l'en li disoit, si que ele en plourent forment souvent et en estoit mout mesaisiee. Ele ot devotion de requerre nostre sainte dame et fu en oraisons a sa tumbe par neuf jours, et de jour en jour ele amendet et au neuvime jour ele fu tout guerie.

[20] Seur Ysabel de Crecy dit en verité que ele estoit mout griément malade et en peril de mort d'une enflure qui la tenoit entour les flans si forment que ele ne se poet drecier; chose que l'en li feyt ne la poet alegier. Les sereurs li aporterent l'orelier qui avoit esté en la sepulture madame par neuf jours; tantost comme ele le mit sus sa fourcele ele alega et fu guerie de la maladie. Seur Agnes de Harecourt, seur Agnes d'Anery, seur Marguerite de Guyse et plusieurs autres sereurs se recordent bien de cete chose.

[21] Une autre fois icele meymes seur Isabel avoit trop grant doleur en sa fourcele et seur Ade de Rains, qui adonc vivet que madame avoit guerie de son doit, li dit, "Alez a la tumbe madame et prené de la terre qui est sus sa tumbe et en metez sus vostre fourcele et vous serez toute guerie." Icele seur Ysabel dit en verité que //(f. 139r) en l'heure que ele mit de cele terre sus sa fourcele ele fu toute guerie.

[22] Seur Erembour de Cerceles dit en verité que ele estoit trop griément malade, et li tenoit cele doleur desous la mamel si que ele ne poet avoir s'alainne.[251] Ele ot fiance en nostre sainte benoite dame et mere et la requit, et aucune des choses qui avoient esté a la sainte dame ele mist u lieu u la maladie estoit, et tantost ele alega et fu guerie. Plusieurs sereurs virent et sorent[252] cete chose.

[23] Seur Aalis de Mucedent avoit la bouche torte et l'eul et la face et le nes aussi[253] comme de[254] paralisie, et la parole li estoit si empechiee que a paines la poet l'en entendre. Et en cet estat ele fu bien trois semaines ou un mois, et[255] nule chose que l'en li poet fere de fisique ne li poet rien valer. Et

holy lady, his reverend aunt.[13] He was cured, so that he himself later said in front of several sisters that she cured him and said that he remembered it well.

Sister Marguerite of Guise had a twig in one of her eyes. She was in such anguish that she could not open the eye. She entreated Madame to aid her and put on her eye some of the clothes of the blessed saint, and soon she was cured.

Sister Marie of Cambrai had so lost her hearing that she could hardly hear at all and did not know how to respond to what was said to her, so that she cried about it quite often and was very troubled. She had the devotion to entreat our holy lady and was in prayer at her tomb for nine days, and from day to day she improved, and on the ninth day she was completely cured.

Sister Isabelle of Crécy says in truth that she was very seriously ill and in danger of death from an inflammation that took her around her sides so strongly that she could not stand up. Nothing that anyone did could alleviate it. The sisters brought her the pillow that had been in the tomb with Madame for nine days. As soon as she put it on her abdomen, she had relief and was cured of the malady. Sister Agnes of Harcourt, Sister Agnes of Anery, Sister Marguerite of Guise, and several other sisters remember this affair well.

Another time this same Sister Isabelle had a great pain in her abdomen, and Sister Ade of Reims, who was alive then (whose finger Madame had cured), said to her, "Go to the tomb of Madame and take some earth that is over the tomb and put some on your abdomen, and you will be entirely cured." This Sister Isabelle says in truth that at the hour in which she put some of this earth on her abdomen she was entirely cured.

Sister Erembour of Cerceles says in truth that she was very seriously ill and the pain took hold of her below her breast so that she could not get her breath. She believed in our holy blessed lady and mother and entreated her, and she put some of the things that had belonged to the holy lady on the place where her malady was, and soon she had relief and was cured. Several sisters saw and knew of this affair.

Sister Alice of Mucedent had a contorted mouth and eye and face and nose, as though paralyzed, and her speech was so impaired that she could barely be understood, and in this condition she remained for a good three weeks or a month, and nothing that anyone could do for her as far as

adonc il li vint devotion et volenté que ele preyt des choses que ele avoit qui
furent nostre sainte dame et mere et que ele les portat a son col et que ele la
requeyt et alat a sa tumbe. Ele y ala par huit jours fere s'oroison[256] et a l'uy-
time jour[257] ele offrit une chandele de la groissece de son chief et de la
longueur de son visage, et tantost aprés ce ele fu toute guerie et onques puys
n'en fu malade si comme il apert. Et de cete chose seur Agnes d'Anery qui la
gardoit en porte tesmong et mout d'autres sereurs qui la virent malade et
puys aprés la virent[258] toute guerie.

[24] Seur Marie de Tremblay dit en vérité que ele estoit alee esbatre vers
le vivier qui est en nostre meson, et s'assit dessus[259] les quarriaux qui sunt
desus le vivier, et y fut une bone piece pour prendre de l'er, quar ele estoit
mout lassee des offices que ele avoit eu a fere. Et si comme ele estoit ileques,
le quarriau sus quoi ele seet[260] despeça desous li et chey u vivier[261] et brisa la
glace et la seur chey avec li[262] vivier et coula dedens le vivier jusques outre la
çainture et coulet jusques au fons,[263] et il li ramembra de nostre //(f. 139v)
sainte dame. Ele la requeyt mout de cuer et dit, "Ma douce dame, sauvez
moi si vraiiement comme je suis vostre fille!" Et tantost Nostre Segneur la
delivra mervelleusement, si comme cele[264] qui estoit en grant peril de mort,
tantost ele s'en yssit legierement de l'iaue, et dit bien que ele n'ot onques si
grant angoisse ne si grant poour de mort et proposa en son cuer de miux
fere. Plusieurs sereurs virent la grieté que ele avoit quant ele fu yssue de ce
grant peril. Cete chose ele recorda a plusieurs sereurs et trouva l'en le quar-
rel despecié si comme ele avoit dit.

[25] Icete[265] meymes seur Marie de Tremblay gardoit seur Desirree
malade que l'en li avoit ballee a garder. La malade li dit que ele li allat querre
de l'iaue de la fontaine du vivier, et seur Marie li dit que ele avoit trop grant
poeur et trop grant horreur pour ce qu'il estoit nuyt aussi comme au premier
somme. Et toute voyet[266] pour acomplir la volenté de la malade ele prit une
chandele et un pot et y[267] ala. Si comme ele y alet,[268] l'anemi vint encontre li
en semblance d'un chien ver et avoit les iex rouges et estincelans et si
grans[269] et si gros qu'il sembloit que ce fussent iex de vache! Ele avoit si grant
poeur que il li sembloit que tout son cors fut emeu et que l'en li tirat les
cheveus amont, et tousjours il venoit encontre son visage et la destourba si[270]
d'aler que ele ne pot onques aler jusques a l'iaue, ains la convint retourner, et
au retourner ele se segna et le bouta de son bras arrieres et dit, "Pater in
manus tuas commendo spiritum meum." Et en cele heure il se departi de li,

medicine was able to help. And then the devotion and desire came to her that she should take some things that she had which had belonged to our holy lady and mother and that she should put them on her neck and that she should entreat her and go to her tomb. She went there to pray for eight days, and on the eighth day she offered a candle the size of her head and the length of her face, and soon after this she was cured and was never afterward ill, as was apparent. And Sister Agnes of Anery, who watched over her, bears witness to this affair and many other sisters who saw her ill and then saw her entirely cured.

Sister Marie of Tremblay says in truth that she went to amuse herself by the pond which is at our house and sat down on the paving stones that are above the pond and was there for a good while to take the air, because she was very tired from the offices that she had had to perform. And while she was there, the stone on which she was sitting moved from under her and fell into the pond and broke the ice, and the sister fell with it [into] the pond and sank in the pond over her belt and sank to the bottom, and the thought of our holy lady came to her. She entreated her from her very heart and said, "My gentle lady, save me, since I am truly your daughter!" And soon our Lord delivered her wonderfully like one who was in great peril of death. Right away she came easily out of the water and said that she had never suffered such anguish nor had had such great fear of death and promised in her heart to do better. Several sisters saw the pain that she had when she had come out of this great danger. She recounted this affair to several sisters, and the stone was found displaced just as she had said.

This same Sister Marie of Tremblay was watching Sister Desirée, who was ill, whom she had been appointed to watch. The sick woman asked her if she would go for her to get some water from the fountain of the pond, and Sister Marie said to her that she was too afraid since it was night, around the first sleep. And [yet], determined to carry out the wish of the sick woman, she took a candle and a pot and went. As she went there, the enemy came against her in the form of a green dog and had red eyes, glowing and so big and so wide that it seemed that they were the eyes of a cow! She was so afraid that it seemed to her that her whole body was moved and that someone had pulled her hair straight up, and still he came against her face and stopped her from advancing so that she could not get to the water, so she had to turn back. And in turning back she crossed herself and pushed him back with her arm and said, "Father, into your hands I com-

si que ele ne sot qu'il devint. Ele prit son tour a aler a la fontainne de la lavanderie. Et quant ele fut illec a la fontainne, il se mit entre[271] li et le fournel et li salli sur les epaules et la volit estrangler. Ainsi comme ele se retourna pour aler s'en, ele se //(f. 140r) segna et dit, "A, a[272] ma douce dame, deffendez moi de ce dyable si comme je suis vostre fille, et je proumet a Dieu et a Nostre Dame et a vous que je me confesseré generaument et amenderé ma vie!" Et ainsi comme ele volet entrer en la meson u la malade giset, ele chey aussi[273] comme toute pasmee et n'ot onques pooir de fermer l'uys, et li pos que ele tenet en sa main chey et fu brisiez. La malade, qui ne se[274] poet remuer, oet bien les cris que seur Marie criet et li diset, "Segnez vous, segnés vous!" Seur Desirree fu tesmong de cete chose se ele fu en vie. Seur Jehanne de Louvençainnes qui garda grant piece la malade et seur Julienne tesmognent que Seur Desirree leur dit plusieurs fois cete chose en sa vie.

[26] *Soeur Jehanne de Louvetaines dit en verité, que en une grande maladie que elle eut, qui li dura trois mois, elle se voua a madame nostre saincte mere, et li pria mout de coeur que elle priast Nostre Seigneur qu'il la sanast, et disoit ainsi, "Ma douce dame, ma douce mere, je vous prie que vous me donniez sancté: car je croy certainement, que vos merites sont plus grands que la necessité que j'ay." Et ainsi prioit en grandes larmes, et plusieurs fois, et li avint qu'une nuict elle fut mout greisvement malade, en telle maniere que il li sembloit que elle ne peust durer, et appella soeur Mahaut d'Escosse qui la gardoit, et li dict, "Signez moy, et me recommandez a madame nostre benoiste mere," et tantost s'endormit. En ce dormir il li sembloit que elle voyoit madame, et s'agenouilloit devant li, et li faisoit sa priere ainsi comme devant a jointes mains, et madame li respondoit, "Allez a mon frere." Aprés elle li sembloit que elle voyoit mout de gens ainsi comme pelerins aller a la tumbe monseigneur le roy, et li estoit advis que elle n'y pouvoit aller. Pour ce si crioit au roy, "Sire, je crie a vous misericorde, senez moy," et li sembla que elle fut portee a la tumbe monseigneur le roy, et que madame y estoit, et li sembloit que li roy tenoit sa main dextre en haut dessus la tumbe. Et madame li disoit, "Sire, segnez, ou sanez ceste soeur," et il la segna, et li dict, "vous serez guerie dedans huict jours." Et tantost comme elle fut esveillee, elle conta ceste chose a seur Mahaut qui la gardoit, et li dit, "Je suis guerie!" Et c'e[s]t verité que el fut tantost guerie; li convent la vit malade, et vit la santé.*

mend my spirit."[14] And at this moment he departed from her so that she did not know what became of him. She took her walk to go to the fountain of the wash house, and when she was there at the fountain, he placed himself between her and the furnace and leapt on her shoulders and tried to strangle her. As she turned around to escape, she crossed herself and said, "Ah, ah, my gentle lady, protect me from this devil since I am your daughter, and I promise to God and to our Lady and to you that I will make a general confession and amend my life!" And as she tried to enter the house where the sick woman lay, she fell as though fainted away, and she could not even close the door, and the pot that she held in her hand fell and was broken. The sick woman, who could not move, heard the cries that Sister Marie cried and said to her, "Cross yourself, cross yourself!" Sister Desirée would be witness to this matter if she were alive. Sister Jeanne of Louveciennes, who watched the sick woman a long time, and Sister Julienne testify that Sister Desirée told them of this affair several times while she was alive.

Sister Jeanne of Louveciennes says in truth that during one great malady that she had, which lasted three months, she vowed herself to Madame our holy mother and prayed to her with her whole heart that she should pray to our Lord that he should heal her, and she spoke thus, "My gentle lady, my gentle mother, I pray that you give me health, because I truly believe that your merits are greater than my necessity." And she prayed thus with great tears and several times. And it came about that one night she was most gravely ill, in such a manner that it seemed to her that she could not go on, and she called Sister Mahaut of Scotland, who was watching her, and said to her, "Make the sign of the cross over me and commend me to Madame our blessed mother," and soon she was asleep. In this sleep it seemed to her that she saw Madame and kneeled before her and offered her prayer to her as before with joined hands, and Madame responded to her, "Go to my brother." Then it seemed to her that she saw many people as though they were pilgrims going to the tomb of Monseigneur the king, and she found that she could not go, so she cried to the king, "Sire, I cry mercy to you, heal me!" And it seemed to her that she was carried to the tomb of Monseigneur the king and that Madame was there, and it seemed to her that the king held his right hand high above the tomb, and Madame said to him, "Sire, make the sign of the cross or heal this sister," and he signed her with the cross and said to her, "You will be healed within eight

585   [27] *Icelle mesme soeur Jehanne de Louvetaines eut une mout griesve ma-*
ladie, qui li dura bien trois ans, et peu avoit d'esperance de jamais avoir santé pour
la griesveté de la maladie. Elle se voua a madame nostre saincte mere, et li promit
590   *que elle jeusneroit en pain et en eau par trois samedis. Quand elle eut ainsi jeusné*
si dict a nostre saincte dame, "A, a ma douce dame, or ay je jeusné par trois samedis
en pain et en eau qui mout m'ont cousté, et encore ne suis je point confortee." Elle
s'endormit, et li sembla que elle fust portee sur la tumbe madame, et que madame
se seoit sur la tumbe, dont la malade fut un peu espouventee, et li souvint, et dict a
595   *soy mesmes, "C'est celle a qui tu requiers aide." Et sembloit a la soeur que madame*
venoit en contre li, et elle disoit a madame, "Madame, je vous prie que vous
m'aidez envers Nostre Seigneur, et me sanez," et madame la prit entre ses mains,
et li dit, "Allez a mon frere." Adonc il sembloit a la soeur que elle voyoit une pro-
cession de roys mout noblement appareillez, et tous couronnez, et en la fin de
600   *celle procession estoit monseigneur le roy Louÿs. Madame prit la soeur, et la*
mit devant luy, et li dit qu'il la segnat; monseigneur le roy segna la soeur, et li dict,
"Vous serez toute guerie." Et certainement la soeur fut toute guerie, si comme il ap-
parut aprés que toutes virent que elle fut guerie, et onques puis n'eut tache de la
maladie.[275]

605   [28] Il avint a seur Sare de Houpelines que un mout felon chien de
nostre meson, qui mout avoit fet de maux as sereurs, eschapa et li vot sallir
au visage, et ele mit sa main au devant, li chiens la prit par la main et li fit 12
playes en la main et u bras, aprés il la prit par la cuisse delez le genoul et li fit
mout de grans plaiies. Ilec avoit mout de sereurs qui s'efforçaiient de li se-
610   courre, mes eles ne pooient oster le chien de li. Adonc seur Sare requeyt
Nostre Segneur et Nostre Dame et nostre sainte mere madame Ysabel, a qui
ele dit ainsi, "Ma douce mere, me laisserés vous mengier as chiens?" Et tantost li chiens s'en ala de sa volenté et la lessa, et ele demoura mout griément
navree. Aprés ce la cuisse de la seur enfla et aggreva si forment que l'en
615   cuyda que ele deut morir. Et adonc ele demoura par congié toute seule a la
tumbe madame tant comme le convent manga et pria Dieu et Nostre Dame
et madame nostre sainte mere que ele li aydat, et tantost avant que li con-

days." And as soon as she woke up, she recounted this affair to Sister Mahaut, who was watching her, and said to her, "I am cured!" And it is true that she was soon cured. The convent saw her ill and saw her healed.

This same Sister Jeanne of Louveciennes had a very serious malady, which lasted a good three years, and she had little hope of ever having her health because of the gravity of the malady. She vowed herself to Madame our holy mother and promised her that she would fast on bread and water for three Saturdays. When she had thus fasted, she said to our holy lady, "Ah, ah, my gentle lady, though I have fasted for three Saturdays on bread and water, which cost me dearly, still I have no relief." She went to sleep and it seemed to her that she was carried to Madame's tomb and that Madame was seated on the tomb, at which the sick woman was a little frightened, and she remembered and said to herself, "It is she of whom you have requested aid." And it seemed to the sister that Madame came close to her, and she said to Madame, "Madame, I pray that you will aid me with our Lord, and heal me." And Madame took her between her hands and said to her, "Go to my brother." Then it seemed to the sister that she saw a procession of kings most nobly appareled, and all crowned, and at the end of this procession was Monseigneur the king Louis. Madame took the sister and put her before him and said to him that he should sign her. Monseigneur the king signed the sister and said to her, "You will be entirely healed." And certainly the sister was entirely healed, as was apparent afterward, as everyone saw that she was healed and was nevermore touched by this malady.

It happened to Sister Sara of Houpelines that a very mean dog of our house, which had done much harm to the sisters, escaped and wanted to leap on her face, and she put her hand out, [and] the dog took her hand and gave her twelve wounds on the hand and on the arm; then he took her by the thigh next to the knee and gave her many serious wounds. Many sisters were there who tried to help her, but they could not get the dog off her. Then Sister Sara requested the aid of our Lord and our Lady and our holy mother, Madame Isabelle, to whom she spoke thus, "My gentle mother, would you let me be eaten by a dog?" And right away the dog went of its own will and left her, and she remained very gravely wounded. After this the sister's thigh swelled up and worsened so much that it was thought that she would die. And then she remained with permission all alone at the tomb of Madame while the convent ate and prayed to God and our Lady

vens eut mangié ele se sentit alegiee de la grant maladie et[276] de l'enfleure et
est toute guerie. Et ce vit seur Ysabel //(f. 140v) de Tremblay qui la gardoit et
620 plusieurs autres sereurs, et nous le veons que ele est toute guerie.

[29] Plusieurs sereurs ont veu grant clarté plusieurs fois entour la tumbe
nostre sainte dame et mere, entour l'eure de matines et autres choses devotes
qui longues sunt a raconter.

[30] Li brevieres seur Agnes de Paris chey en yaue tout ouvert et fu si du
625 tout moulliés dedens et dehors qu'il ne semblet pas qu'il fut jamés convena-
bles a lire la letre.[277] L'en le porta par devotion sus la tumbe a nostre sainte
dame et le laissa l'en ilec[278] entour trois heures. Il fu restorez en son premier
estat et est biaus et lisables comme devant ce qu'il cheyt en l'yaue.

[31] Cete[279] meymes seur Agnes avoit si mal dedens le conduyt de sa
630 gorge que ele en[280] estoit mout effree. Si tost comme elle ot mys sus le mal
aucunes des choses qui avoient touchié au saint cors de madame, ele rendi
par la bouche aussi[281] comme palu et fu nettement guerie.

[32] Nous ne[282] porriens raconter a bries paroles les biens et les consolations espirituex que ele a fet as persones qui devotement l'ont requeys a[283]
635 ayde. De queconque tribulation et mesese l'en la requiert ele secourt et con-
forte ysnelement qui de vrai cuer la prie.

[33] Une femme de Paris qui a non Agnes[284] la Coffriere avoit .i.[285]
enfant mout griément malade et n'i atendet l'en que la mort. Ele l'amoit
mout, quar ele n'avoit plus d'enfans. Ele et autres persones avoient vellé
640 devant l'enfant, pour ce que l'en atendoit sa fin. L'en la fit aler reposer.
Ele s'en dormi et en ce dormir il li sembla que ele oÿ une voix qui li dit,
"Agnes, voe ton enfant a madame Ysabel pres de Saint Clo et li offre
le hennab que ton pere te donna, //(f. 141r) et ton enfant sera gueris." L'en-
demain ele vint en nostre meson en pelerinage et offrit le hennab et li enfens
645 fu gueris.

[34] Une femme de Surenes[286] qui a non Agnes perdi la vue de ses
iex par force de maladie. Ele se fit amener a nostre abeÿe et se voua a nostre sainte dame et li proumit deux iex de cire. Si tost comme ele ot fet
son veu et s'oraison[287] u moutier, ele vit et en ce jour ele receut plainnement
650 sa[288] vue.

and Madame our holy mother that she would aid her. And immediately, before the convent had eaten, she felt relieved of the great malady and of the swelling and was entirely cured. And Sister Isabelle of Tremblay, who was guarding her, saw this and several other sisters, and we see that she is entirely cured.

Several sisters have seen a great light several times around the tomb of our holy lady and mother at the hour of matins and other devout things that would take a long time to recount.

The breviary of Sister Agnes of Paris fell into the water completely open and was so completely soaked inside and out that it did not seem that it would ever be possible to read the letters. Out of devotion it was carried above the tomb of our holy lady and left there for three hours. It was restored to its original state and is as beautiful and readable as it was before it had fallen into the water.

This same Sister Agnes had such a pain in her throat that she was very frightened by it. As soon as she had placed on the pain some things that had touched the holy body of Madame, she emitted from her mouth a sort of mud and was completely cured.

We would not be able to recount in a few words the spiritual good and consolations that she has provided to people who have devoutly requested her aid. In any tribulation and unhappiness in which she is asked for help, she promptly aids and comforts whoever prays to her with a true heart.

A woman of Paris, who is named Agnes "the chest maker," had a child who was very seriously ill, and it was expected that it would die. She loved it very much, because she did not have any other children. She and other people had kept a vigil by the child, since its end was expected. They made her go and lie down. She fell asleep, and in her sleep it seemed to her that she heard a voice which said to her, "Agnes, dedicate your child to Madame Isabelle, near St. Cloud, and offer her the cup that your father gave you, and your child will be cured." The next day she came to our house on pilgrimage and offered the cup, and the child was cured.

A woman from Suresnes, who is named Agnes, lost the sight in her eyes because of a malady. She had herself led to our abbey and dedicated herself to our holy lady and promised her two eyes made of wax. As soon as she had made her vow and prayer at the church, she saw, and on this day she fully received her sight.

[35] Une pucele qui estoit deux luyes loins de nostre eglise estoit en peril de perdre sa virginité, et la nuyt avant que ele fu livree nostre sainte dame li aparut en son[289] dormant et li dit, "Lieve sus, va a m'abeÿe qui est pres de Saint Clo et tu sera delivree." La pucele se leva tres matin et comme ele ne seut quel[290] part l'abaÿe fut, ele acourut tout dret et vint si suant et si lassee de courre que a painnes poet ele avoir s'alainne. Et pour le grant desirrier que ele avoit d'estre sauvee ele lessa son sercot u boias pour plustost acourre, et li fu[291] sercos trouvé si comme Diex vot. Et d'ilec en avant la pucele parmaint[292] en sa netee et mena bele vie et honeste, si comme tesmognent les personnes entre qui ele demoura.

[36] Deux hommes devers Tournay vindrent a nostre abeÿe et apporterent a offrande[293] deux chandeles de leur lonc, et requirent que l'en leur monstrat la tumbe nostre sainte dame. Et dirent que il estoient en prison et en peril de la mort de la hart,[294] et une voix leur dit, "Vouez vous a madame Ysabel[295] pres de Saint Clo et vous serés delivrez."[296] Pour ce il estoient venus et requeroient a grant instance a voiar la tumbe de la benoite dame. En leur respondi qu'il n'estoit pas acoustumé d'ouvrir souvent la fenestre. En fit arder leurs chandeles entour la tumbe et il s'en[297] ralerent tous delivrez.

[37] La guete de nostre meson neet le moutier et estoit en haut //(f. 141v) as voutes en une corbelle tiree a cordes par engin. La corde rompi et il cheyt sur les estaus du moutier et fu mout quassez et ot une plaie en son chief de ce qui se bleça au chaair, et fu mervelles qu'i[298] ne fu tous ecervelez. Et douta l'en qu'il ne morut, et convint les freres venir en[299] grant hate pour lui confesser. Les sereurs en orent mout grant pitié et le vouerent a madame nostre sainte mere, et dedens brief tans[300] il fu tous gueris et n'ot nul mahaing de la bleceure.

[38] Quant madame la reyne demouroit en notre meson, li vallés a son aumosnier fu malades et chey en forte frenaisie. Bones gens orent pitié de[301] lui et le vouerent a madame nostre sainte dame et mere et li offrirent une chandele du lonc au malade. Tantost li malades revint en[302] son sens et fu gueris de la frenaisie et se confessa et s'aparella. Ce virent li frere de nostre meson et plusieurs autres gens.

[39] Phelippe procureur de nostre abeÿe avoit fievre tiercenne si apre et si fort[303] que l'en doutet qu'il ne perdit son sens. Il ne poet suer pour riens

A maiden who was two leagues distant from our church was in danger of losing her virginity, and the night before she would have given herself up, our holy lady appeared to her in her sleep and said to her, "Get up, go to my abbey, which is near St. Cloud, and you will be delivered." The maiden got up very early, and though she did not know where the abbey was, she ran right to it and arrived sweating so much and so tired from running that she could barely catch her breath. And out of the great desire that she had to be saved she left her outer coat in the woods to be able to run faster, and the coat was found just as God wished. And from then on the maiden remained in her purity and led a good and honest life, as the people among whom she lived testify.

Two men from around Tournai came to our abbey and brought an offering of two candles of their own height and asked that they be shown the tomb of our holy lady. And they said that they had been in prison and in danger of death by the noose and a voice told them, "Dedicate yourselves to Madame Isabelle, near St. Cloud, and you will be delivered!" For this reason they had come and asked very insistently to see the tomb of the blessed lady. We told them that we were not accustomed to open the window very often. Their candles were lit around the tomb, and they departed entirely delivered.

The sentinel of our house was cleaning the church and was high in the vaults in a basket pulled by a cord by machine. The cord broke, and he fell on the stalls of the church and was badly broken and had a wound on his head, which was injured in the fall, and it was amazing that he did not have his brains entirely dashed out. And it was thought that he would die, and the brothers had to come in great haste to confess him. The sisters had great pity for him and dedicated him to Madame our holy mother, and within a brief time he was entirely cured and suffered no mutilation from his injury.

When Madame the queen was staying at our house, the valet of her chaplain was ill and fell into a great frenzy. Some good people had pity on him and dedicated him to Madame our holy lady and mother and offered her a candle of the height of the sick man. Soon the sick man returned to his senses and was cured of his frenzy and confessed himself and dressed himself. The brothers of our house saw this and several other people.

Philip, the procurator of our abbey, had a tertian fever so intense and so strong that it was thought that he would lose his senses. He could not

que l'en li feyt. Si tost comme l'en le coucha sus l'orelier que madame nostre sainte[304] mere ot en sous son chief, tantost il sua et fu tous gueris.

[40] Li fix Richart le galois,[305] aprés ce qu'il ot eu sus soi[306] de la terre qui fu prise entour la sepulture de la sainte dame, fu gueris de fievre cotidiane
690 que il avoit eu grant piece.

XL Miracles
Fin

5 Janvier 1653

sweat, no matter what was tried. As soon as he was laid on the pillow that Madame our holy mother had had under her head, he sweated and was entirely cured.

The son of Richard the Welshman, after he had had on him some of the earth that was taken from around the grave of the holy lady, was cured of a quotidien fever[15] that he had had for a long while.

Forty miracles

The End
5 January 1653[16]

Notes

Notes to Edition

1. *Heading added by* T2. *Last sentence in right margin.*
2. la *add.* D.
3. sainte *corr. to* cette P2.
4. *om.* D, P2.
5. nous *add.* P2.
6. Cette P2.
7. vie P2.
8. grand P2.
9. sainteté de vie P2.
10. il *add.* D, P2.
11. penitance D.
12. chasteté T1; *corr. to* chasteé T2; chasteté D.
13. fut T1; *corr. to* fu *[probably]* T2.
14. *om.* T1; *add.* T2.
15. approchez T1; *corr. to* apprenez T2; approchez, apprenez D; P (Perrier) *stops transcription to debate this reading. After a lacuna where his discussion is lost,* P *resumes,* "qui est le terme propre de l'Evangile, et qui vaut mieux que 'approchier' qui est faux et impropre." *It seems evident that there was some confusion at this point in Agnes's original manuscript.*
16. Icelle D; Icette P1.
17. Isabelle de France D.
18. heures T1; *corr. to* heuvres *[probably]* T2.
19. *om.* D.
20. ces P1.
21. P1 *and* P2 *end here.*
22. *om.* D.
23. voluntiers *corr. to* voulentiers T1.
24. que l'en li feit pour faire T1; *negation marks under* faire *[probably] add.* T2; que l'on ly peut faire D.
25. et haults *om. with space left* T1; U te T2; *corr. to* U tans T2.
26. *om. with space left* T1; *text supplied from* D.
27. conjurée D.
28. *om. with space left* T1; *add.* T2; heritier D.
29. s'en vout *om. with space left* T1; *add.* T2.
30. en parfait virginité *om.* T1; *add.* T2.

31. *sic* T1; le Pape D.
32. de T1; *corr. to* a T2; de D.
33. si D.
34. pourtez T1; *corr. to* pourfis T2.
35. viennent T1; *corr. to* viennet T2.
36. telle D.
37. *om.* D.
38. y D.
39. une autre lettre, par laquelle D.
40. de T1; *corr. to* a T2; de D.
41. bon T1; *corr. to* boen T2.
42. les D.
43. Madame D.
44. *om. with space left* T1; *add.* T2.
45. Je suer Agnes de harcourt oï *om. with space left* T1; *add.* T2.
46. é je *om. with space left* T1; *add.* T2.
47. *om. with space left* T1; *add.* T2.
48. convient T1; *corr. to* convint T2.
49. et on s'en alla D *for* et envoia l'en.
50. *add. above line* T1.
51. *om. with space left* T1; en ananterre *add.* T2 [*for* a Nanterre?]; en Angleterre D.
52. *om. with space left* T1; a certes *add.* T2.
53. contrainlir [?] T1; *corr. to* contrainsit T2.
54. *om. with space left* T1; *add.* T2.
55. *om. with space left* T1; *add.* T2; Madame *add.* D.
56. levoit [?] T1; *corr. to* seroit T1.
57. *illeg.* T1; *corr. to* despisoit T2.
58. *illeg.* T1; *corr. to* acquere T2.
59. si T1; *corr. to* li T2.
60. grand T1; *corr. to* grant T2.
61. *om. with space left* T1; *add.* T2.
62. *om. with space left* T1; *add.* T2.
63. avenoit T1; *corr. to* avenit T2.
64. fois T1; *corr. to* fais T2.
65. *om.* D.
66. *om. with space left* T1; reerecroient *add.* T2, *then corr. to* recroient T2; re-
querroient D.
67. soeur T1; *corr. to* seur T2.
68. *om. with space left* T1; *add.* T2.

69. *om.* D.

70. estant T1; *corr. to* estait T2.

71. *illeg.* T1; *corr. to* reponnoit T2.

72. *om. with space left* T1; *add.* T2.

73. hirer que ces qui devoit trousser et emmaler *om. with space left* T1; *add.* T2.

74. ylesquelz T1; *corr. to* ylesques T2.

75. sez cria T1; *corr. to* s'escria T2.

76. ja coururent T1; *corr. to* i acoururent T2.

77. Monseigneur le Roy sainct Louys D.

78. *om. with space left* T1; *add.* T2.

79. Elle mesme T1; *corr. to* icele mesme T2.

80. *Hand one* (T1) *ends. Hand two* (T2) *begins.*

81. de D.

82. dame D.

83. ne *add.* T2.

84. ju *corr. to* geunoit T2.

85. manger D.

86. feis [?] *corr. to* feist T2.

87. *illeg.*; *corr. to* envoiet T2.

88. aumosne *corr. to* aumone T2.

89. merveilleusement *corr. to* mervilleusement T2.

90. deligamment et l'escoutoit tout mout *om.* D.

91. grande *corr. to* grant T2.

92. Evangiles *corr. to* Euvangiles T2.

93. *illeg.*; *corr. to* oiet T2.

94. revanment T2; reveremment D.

95. me dites T2; m'a dit D.

96. tans *corr. to* leus T2; temps D.

97. pournient *corr. to* pour nient T2.

98. une *add.* T2.

99. dame D.

100. tousjours avoit D.

101. telle D.

102. *illeg.*; *corr. to* et li T2.

103. souvent *del.* T2; et *add.* D.

104. do *corr. to* denoit T2.

105. dames *corr. to* dame T2; dames D.

106. salut *corr. to* salu T2.

107. du salut D.

108. n'eut dict D.

109. par les *for* yces D.

110. en l'Evangile *om.* D.

111. poures *corr. to* pouvres; il faut propres *add. in parenthesis* T2.

112. rel *corr. to* regligeus T2.

113. qu'en *corr. to* c'one les, *then corr. to* c'on ne les T2.

114. pitiet *corr. to* pities [?] T2.

115. couvrechief *corr. to* cueurechief T2.

116. et li dit *add. above line* T2.

117. pria et *add. above line* T2.

118. secretment *corr. to* secreement T2.

119. des *corr. to* de T2; des D.

120. la chacerent *corr. to* l'achaterent T2; l'achepterent D.

121. qui mourut en Montpencier *add. above line* T2; *om.* D.

122. lequel *for* ce qu'ele D.

123. comparaison *corr. to* comparissons T2.

124. maison *corr. to* meson T2.

125. *om.* D.

126. choscex *corr. to* chosce T2.

127. *sic* T2, D.

128. Bonavanture *corr. to* Bone avanture, *then corr. to* Bone aventure T2.

129. ez *corr. to* es T2.

130. privileges *corr. to* previleges T2.

131. est *corr. to* estoit T2.

132. peines *corr. to* painnes T2.

133. *om. with space left* D.

134. le *corr. to* li T2.

135. aux *corr. to* as T2.

136. *sic* T1; *om.* D.

137. l'apostoile *corr. to* l'apoitoile T2; du Pape D.

138. souffrire *corr. to* souffire T2.

139. le *add.* D.

140. Je *corr. to* Et T2.

141. pouq *corr. to* pourcoi T2.

142. nostre D.

143. qu'il *corr. to* qu'i T2.

144. auquel D.

145. par *corr. to* Par T2.

146. non plus *for* neys D.

147. qu'elle *corr. to* qu'ele T2.

148. les lettres et les D.
149. *add. above line* T2.
150. ce D.
151. *sic* T2, D.
152. il faut *for* y fust D.
153. partissiez D.
154. il D.
155. que c'estoit *om.* D.
156. de *add.* D.
157. *sic* [*for* pardurable?] T2; perpetuele D.
158. *sic* [*for* cremoit?] T2; craignoit D.
159. a prié *corr. to* apoié T2.
160. devant *add.* T2.
161. qu'ils D.
162. qui D.
163. luy sembloit *corr. to* li sambloit T2.
164. voir *corr. to* l'oir T2.
165. pecheur *corr. to* picheur T2.
166. en terre D.
167. *om.* D.
168. ce D.
169. si D.
170. il eust peché ou il n'y en *for* il n'i eust pichiez neys ou il n'en D.
171. Et en sa fin *corr. to* Et ot sa fin T2; Elle eut en sa fin D.
172. tres-grandes D.
173. *om.* D.
174. *add. above line* T2.
175. *om.* D.
176. ces *corr. to* tiex T2.
177. pour D.
178. Raucedent *corr. to* Mucedent T2.
179. prias *corr. to* priat T2.
180. ge *corr. to* guerie T2.
181. la D.
182. tesmoing *corr. to* tesmong T2.
183. tesmoing *corr. to* tesmong T2.
184. cette *corr. to* cete T2.
185. *illeg.; corr. to* u T2.
186. Clemence *corr. to* Climence T2.
187. dit en verité *add. above line* T2.

188. pres de D.

189. por savoir *add. above line* T2.

190. aucune D.

191. Court *corr. to* court T2.

192. o *corr. to* u T2.

193. *om.* D.

194. *illeg.; del.* T2.

195. qui D.

196. *om.* D.

197. et *add.* D.

198. yeux *corr. to* eus T2.

199. traitions *corr. to* traitiens T2.

200. la dame d'Audenard et dame Huloys la veufue, et plusiers autres personnes bourgeoises de Paris D.

201. Guise D.

202. li *corr. to* ii, *then corr. to* 2 T2.

203. avec *add.* D.

204. Pierre de Ville D.

205. *illeg.; del.* T2.

206. ils *corr. to* il T2.

207. Le frere Denys *for* Icis freres D.

208. *om.* D.

209. sont D.

210. tesmoing *corr. to* tesmong T2 [// *add.* T2].

211. *illeg.; del.* T2.

212. tesmoing *corr. to* tesmong T2.

213. emporta D.

214. *illeg.; corr. to* neuf T2.

215. qu il n'y D.

216. *om.* D.

217. si *del.* T2.

218. *add. above line* T2.

219. il *add.* D.

220. *sic* T2; joint D.

221. aussi *for* au darrenier D.

222. s'endormit *corr. to* s'endormi T2.

223. de D.

224. de Escosse *corr. to* d'Escoce T2.

225. *om.* D.

226. quand D.

227. les *add.* D.

228. *illeg.; del.* T2.

229. *illeg.; corr. to* les T2.

230. *illeg.; del.* T2.

231. mengoit *corr. to* menget T2.

232. pour D.

233. *illeg.; del.* T2.

234. table *corr. to* tumbe T2.

235. saner D.

236. lavoit *corr. to* avoit T2.

237. grande *add.* D.

238. ha *corr. to* hennab T2.

239. eus *corr. to* ot T2.

240. à *add.* D.

241. prom *corr. to* proumit T2; à ambes deux *add.* D.

242. eu *corr. to* ot T2.

243. fai *corr. to* fere T2.

244. du *corr. to* au T2.

245. qu'il D.

246. guerit *corr. to* gueri T2.

247. li en D.

248. [*// add.* T2.]

249. ainsi D.

250. geute *corr. to* goute T2.

251. s'alaine *corr. to* s'alainne T2; l'halaine D.

252. asseurent D.

253. ainsi D.

254. des *del.* T2.

255. et *om.* D.

256. l'oraison D.

257. *add. above line* T2.

258. malade et puys aprés la virent *om.* D.

259. sus D.

260. se debat D.

261. *illeg.; corr. to* u vivier T2.

262. au D.

263. fond *corr. to* fons T2.

264. elle D.

265. Icelle D.

266. preste D.

267. *illeg.; corr. to* y T2.
268. le *del.* T2.
269. grant *corr. to* grans T2.
270. li D.
271. outre D.
272. *om.* D.
273. ainsi D.
274. s'en D.
275. *Miracles 26 and 27 om.* T2; *supplied from* D.
276. *om.* D.
277. lettre *corr. to* letre T2.
278. illec *corr. to* ilec T2.
279. Icelle D.
280. *om.* D.
281. ainsi D.
282. *om.* D.
283. *om.* D.
284. *add. above line* T2.
285. un *corr. to* .i. T2.
286. Suresnes *corr. to* Surenes T2.
287. l'oraison D.
288. la D.
289. *om.* D.
290. quele *corr. to* quel T2.
291. fut li D.
292. demeura D.
293. l'offrande D.
294. corde D.
295. Isabel *corr. to* Ysabel T2.
296. et *add.* D.
297. ils en D.
298. qu'il D.
299. a D.
300. ten *corr. to* tans T2.
301. lu *corr. to* lui T2.
302. a *corr. to* en T2.
303. et si fort *om.* D.
304. dame et *del.* T2.
305. le galois *om.* D.
306. son *corr. to* soi T2.

1. Matthew 11:29.
2. Ecclesiasticus 3:20.
3. Du Cange's edition for this passage substituted "conjurée" for "jurée," which was followed by the Bollandist Latin translation as "Sollicitata fuit conjunctis amicorum precibus," to give the sense of "urged by her friends." In this period, however, "jurée" not only had the modern sense of "sworn," "promised," or "pledged," but also literally "betrothed," and so is an inherently likely reading. In this case, "amis" must take on the sense of "kinsmen," or "family." See, for example, Alan Hindley, Frederick W. Langley, and Brian J. Levy, *Old French–English Dictionary* (Cambridge: Cambridge University Press, 2000), which for "jurer" gives "swear, swear by, declare on oath, promise, betroth, curse," and for "ami" lists "friend, kinsman, lover, beloved" as the range of meanings.
4. This seems the most likely interpretation of Agnes's text. Saint-Germain-en-Laye is twenty kilometers west of modern Paris, and the town of Nanterre lies in between. Thus it seems more likely that Blanche would write to this nearby location than to far-off England (*Angleterre*).
5. Fréderic Godefroy, *Dictionnaire de l'ancienne langue française*, vol. 4 (Paris, 1885), 134, gives a specifically Norman usage for "fregon" (alternative spellings "fracon, fraijon, fragon") as "arbrisseau dont les feuilles extrêmement aigües ont la forme exacte d'un fer de lance" (a shrub whose extremely sharp leaves have the exact form of the tip of a lance). This definition seems likely to give the sense of Agnes's reference.
6. Cf. Matthew 6:1–4; 25:35–46.
7. This translation assumes that the redundant "laquele qui cousta" should read "laquele li cousta."
8. Cf. Luke 1:48.
9. A fever that recurs every third day, counting both days of occurrence.
10. Godefroy, *Dictionnaire*, 5:635, cites Agnes of Harcourt's text as the sole example of this term.
11. A fever that recurs every fourth day, counting both days of occurrence.
12. Cf. Psalms 75:3.
13. Isabelle was actually the great-aunt of the future Philip IV.
14. Psalms 30:6; Luke 23:46.
15. A fever that recurs every day.
16. The date on which Antoine Le Maistre finished his copy.

Index to the Introduction & Translations

Abbey of the Humility of Our Lady (Abbeye de l'Humilité de Notre Dame; Longchamp), 2–8
  Capetians and, 16–17
  founding of, 47, 65
  name of, 67
  pilgrimage and, 17
  sentinel of, 91
Ade of Reims, Sister, 77, 81
Adrian V, Pope, 11
Agnes of Anery, Sister (abbess of Longchamp), 6n8, 71, 77, 81, 83
Agnes the "chestmaker" (la Coffriere, of Paris), 17, 89
child of, 89
Agnes of Harcourt, Sister (abbess of Longchamp) 1–3, 9, 28, 47, 50n1, 53–63, 67, 69, 71, 77, 81
  biography of, 3–8
  birth of, 6
  books of, 7–8
  Capetian sanctity and, 11–15
  death of, 7
  manuscripts containing works of, 24–36
  motivations for writing, 15–17

portrayal of Isabelle of France, 20–24
  seal of, 8, 8n14
  and women's writing, 17–20
Agnes of Paris, Sister, 89
Agnes of Suresnes, 17
Alexander IV, Pope, 2–3, 34, 47
Alice of Mucedent, Sister, 71, 81
Alix of Beaumont, 4
Alfonso VIII (king of Castile), 16, 53
Alphonse of Poitiers (brother of Isabelle of France), 14
Angela of Foligno, 18–19
Angre, Sister, 47, 50n1
Audenarde, the Lady of, 75
Aveline of Hainault, Sister, 73
Aymeric of Veire (chancellor of Notre Dame), 22, 30, 65

Baudonivia, 19n32
Beatrice of Nazareth, 18
Beguines, 18, 18n29
Benedict Gaietani. See Boniface VIII
Blanche of Castile (mother of Isabelle of France), 2, 14, 17, 53, 55, 57, 59

Bonaventure, Saint (Franciscan
  Minister General and Master
  at Paris), 3, 23, 65
Boniface VIII, Pope, 14n23
Brabant, Duchess of, 75

Charles of Anjou (king of Sicily,
  brother of Isabelle of France),
  9–11, 10nn15–16, 11n18, 16, 53
  and Capetian sanctity, 13–14, 14n23
Charles of Valois, 4
Clare, Saint, 12, 18–19, 34n65, 47
Clemence of Argas, Sister, 73
Clemence of Barking, 19, 19n33
Cocheris, Hippolyte, 26–27nn44–45
Conrad IV (king of Germany, son of
  Frederick II), 2, 55

d'Alençon, Ubald, 27n45
de Boissy, Adrian, 33
de La Chaise, Filleau, 36
Denis of Etampes, Brother, 73
Desirée, Sister, 83–85
Douceline of Digne, 19
Du Cange, Charles, 24, 29–32
Duchesne, Gaston, 26–27n45

Erembour of Cerceles, Sister, 73, 81
Ermengarde of Chartres, Sister, 79
Ermesent of Paris, Sister, 77
Eudes of Rosny, Brother (Franciscan
  Master at Paris), 3, 23, 65, 69, 75

Felipa of Porcellet, 19–20, 19n31
Francis, Saint, 12, 34n65, 47
Frederick II (emperor), 2, 55

Geoffrey of Vierson, Brother (Franciscan Master at Paris), 23, 65

Giles of Sally, Brother, 75–77
Gregory X, Pope, 11
Grundmann, Herbert, 18
Guy of Harcourt, 4

Hadewijch of Brabant, 18–19
Helen of Buisement, 16, 59, 61–63
Heloise (female author), 17
Helois, bourgeois widow of Paris, 75
Hérouval, Antoine Vyon de, 28n49, 29,
  29n52, 32, 33n60
Hildegard of Bingen, 17, 19n32
Hugh of Lusignan (count of
  La Marche), 2

Innocent IV, Pope, 2, 55
Innocent V, Pope, 11
Innocent XII, Pope, 25n41
Isabelle of Angoulême (countess of
  La Marche), 2
Isabelle of Crécy, Sister, 81
Isabelle of France, 16, 33, 35, 35n68, 47,
  49, 50n1
  biography of, 2–3
  and Capetian sanctity, 13–15
  character of, 23
  charity of, 59, 63, 65
  confession and, 61
  crusades and, 65
  damsels of, 57, 59, 61
  death of, 3, 12, 21, 49, 69, 73–75, 79
  disciplines of, 61–63
  dress of, 55, 57
  food and, 59, 63
  education of, 55
  epitaph of, 36, 36n73
  humility of, 55, 67, 69
  illness and, 57, 67, 69
  Latin knowledge of, 23, 61

love of truth of, 57–59, 63
miracles of, 70–93
and prayer, 59, 61
relationship to Agnes of Harcourt
of, 5
relics of, 57, 75
representation of in Agnes of
Harcourt's writings, 15–17, 21–24
rules of, 3, 11, 21, 23, 30, 65–67
silence of, 59, 69
translation of, 73–75
youth of, 53–59
Isabelle of Tremblay, Sister, 89
Isabelle of Venice of Reims, Sister
(President of Longchamp), 6n8,
47, 50n1

Jean I of Harcourt, 3–4, 7n10
Jean II of Harcourt, 4
Jeanne, Lady, 65
Jeanne of Grece (abbess of
Longchamp), 6n8
Jeanne of Harcourt, the Elder, 4
Jeanne of Harcourt, the Younger
(abbess of Longchamp), 4–5, 7n10
Jeanne of Louveciennes, Sister, 38n76,
73, 85–87
Jeanne of Nevers (abbess of
Longchamp), 6n8
John XXI, Pope, 11
Joyenval, monastery of, 8
Julienne, Sister, 47, 50n1, 79, 85
Julianne of Troyes (abbess of
Longchamp), 6n8

Le Maistre, Antoine, 27–33,
27–28nn48–49, 37–40, 38n75,
102n16
Leo X, Pope, 3, 33

Letter on Louis IX and Longchamp, 1, 6n8
date of, 9
editorial principles for, 37
interest of, 21
language of, 40–41
and Louis IX's canonization, 12–13,
15, 21
manuscripts of, 33–36
text of, 46–49
Life of Isabelle of France, 1–2, 5, 13
audiences of, 15–17
date of, 9–10
Du Cange's edition of, 24n39, 29–33
editorial principles for, 37–40
language of, 41
original manuscript of, 25–27, 53
structure of, 21
text of, 52–93
Tillemont's manuscript of, 27–28
Longchamp. See Abbey of the
Humility of Our Lady
Louis VIII (king of France, father of
Isabelle of France), 2, 53, 65
Louis IX (king of France, St. Louis),
2–4, 10n15, 16, 21, 23, 35n68, 47, 49,
50n1, 53, 57, 59, 63, 67, 71
canonization process of, 11–15
gifts to Longchamp, 49
in miracles with Isabelle of France,
79, 85–87
preaching of, 47–49
sergeant of, 71
Louis (oldest son of Louis IX), 35n68,
47, 50n1

Mahaut of Gondarville, Sister, 47,
50n1, 59
Mahaut of Guyencourt (abbess of
Longchamp), 6n8

Mahaut of Scotland, Sister, 77, 85–87
Marguerite of Constantinople
    (countess of Flanders), 75
Marguerite of Guise, Sister, 81
Marguerite La Gencienne, Sister,
    34n64
Marguerite of Oingt, 20, 20n34
Marguerite Porete, 18–20
Marguerite of Provence (wife of Louis
    IX), 10n15, 16, 21, 35n68, 47, 50n1,
    57, 71, 79, 91
  chaplain of, 91
  valet of, 91
Marie of Cambrai, Sister, 77, 81
Marie of Flanders (Cistercian nun),
    75
Marie of France, 17, 19–20, 20n33
Marie of Tremblay, Sister, 77, 83, 85
Martin IV, Pope, 11–12
Mechthild of Magdeburg, 18–19
Meru, the damsel of, 63

Nanterre, town of, 57, 102n4
Nicholas III, Pope, 11

Paris, Paulin, 1, 1n1, 27n44
Peronelle of Montfort, Lady, 65
Perrier, Pierre, 25, 25n41, 26nn44–45,
    34–35, 38–39, 50n1
Pierre of Meureville, Brother, 75
Philip II Augustus (king of France,
    grandfather of Isabelle of France),
    16, 53
Philip III (king of France) 4, 9–10,
    10n15, 79
Philip IV (king of France) 4, 10n15,
    16–17, 21, 79–81
Philip (procurator of Longchamp),
    91–93

Raoul of Harcourt, 4
Richard the Welshman, 93
  son of, 93
Robert of Artois (brother of Isabelle
    of France), 14
Robert of Harcourt, 4
Roulliard, Sébastien, 36

Saint Antoine, nunnery of, 65
Saint Cloud, town of, 17, 25n41, 35n68,
    89, 91
Saint Denis, monastery of, 8, 11–12
Saint Geneviève, monastery of, 8
Saint Germain-en-Laye, monastery
    of, 57
Saint Victor, monastery of, 8
Sara of Houpelines, Sister, 71, 87
Simon of Brie. *See* Martin IV
Souciet, Stephan, 25, 25n42

Thomas of Plexi, Brother, 75
Tillemont, Sébastian le Nain de, 13n20,
    27–28, 27n46, 29, 36–37, 38n75
Trouillard, Guy, 26n44

Urban IV, Pope, 3

Vauchez, André, 13
*Vie d'Isabelle de France. See Life of
    Isabelle of France*

William of Harcombourg, Brother
    (Franciscan Provincial Minister of
    France and Master at Paris), 3, 23,
    35n68, 65
William of Meliton, Brother (Francis-
    can Master at Paris), 3, 23, 65
William of Quitry (canon of Vernon),
    75

SEAN L. FIELD
is assistant professor of history at the University of Vermont.